Exciting Nev

CW00742243

Dear Readers,

We are excited to announce major updates in this new edition of the book (fifth edition):

- This updated edition contains two new chapters on the Accounting Cycle.

- The chapter contents have been fully updated and reflect the current best -practices within the world of financial accounting. This book approaches financial accounting from both an academic and professional perspective.

- The chapter questions have been fully updated and additional problem-based exercises have been created to mirror real-world problems that many professionals face in the workforce. This 5th edition also contains many case studies that reflect real-life issues.

- The chapter summaries have been fully evaluated to ensure that they provide only the most crucial components covered in the body of each chapter.

- This 5th edition has more content coverage, which will appeal to modern students wanting the most up-to-date information about the accounting world.

THIS BOOK IS AVAILABLE IN E-BOOK, PAPERBACK AND HARDBACK (COLOR) FORMAT.

SELF-LEARNING MANAGEMENT SERIES

TITLE	PAPERBACK* ISBN
AGILE ESSENTIALS	9781636510057
BUSINESS PLAN ESSENTIALS	9781636511214
BUSINESS STRATEGY ESSENTIALS	9781949395778
COST ACCOUNTING AND MANAGEMENT ESSENTIALS	9781636511030
DATA ANALYTICS ESSENTIALS	9781636511184
DECISION MAKING ESSENTIALS	9781636510026
DIGITAL MARKETING ESSENTIALS	9781949395747
DIVERSITY IN THE WORKPLACE ESSENTIALS	9781636511122
FINANCIAL ACCOUNTING ESSENTIALS	9781636510972
FINANCIAL MANAGEMENT ESSENTIALS	9781636511009
HR ANALYTICS ESSENTIALS	9781636510347
HUMAN RESOURCE MANAGEMENT ESSENTIALS	9781949395839
LEADERSHIP ESSENTIALS	9781636510316
MARKETING MANAGEMENT ESSENTIALS	9781949395792
MICROECONOMICS ESSENTIALS	9781636511153
OPERATIONS AND SUPPLY CHAIN MANAGEMENT ESSENTIALS	9781949395242
ORGANIZATIONAL BEHAVIOR ESSENTIALS	9781636510378
PRINCIPLES OF MANAGEMENT ESSENTIALS	9781949395662
PROJECT MANAGEMENT ESSENTIALS	9781636510712
SALES MANAGEMENT ESSENTIALS	9781636510743

*Also available in Hardback & Ebook formats

BUY 3 FOR THE PRICE OF 2

USE DISCOUNT CODE 3FOR2

Offer valid only on

www.vibrantpublishers.com

SELF-LEARNING MANAGEMENT SERIES

FINANCIAL ACCOUNTING ESSENTIALS

YOU ALWAYS WANTED TO KNOW

FIFTH EDITION

A simple guide to understanding complex financial statements

KALPESH ASHAR

Financial Accounting Essentials You Always Wanted To Know

Fifth Edition

Paperback ISBN 10: 1-63651-097-3
Paperback ISBN 13: 978-1-63651-097-2

Ebook ISBN 10: 1-63651-098-1
Ebook ISBN 13: 978-1-63651-098-9

Hardback ISBN 10: 1-63651-099-X
Hardback ISBN 13: 978-1-63651-099-6

Library of Congress Control Number: 2011927075

This publication is designed to provide accurate and authoritative information in regard to the subject matter covered. The Author has made every effort in the preparation of this book to ensure the accuracy of the information. However, information in this book is sold without warranty either expressed or implied. The Author or the Publisher will not be liable for any damages caused or alleged to be caused either directly or indirectly by this book.

Vibrant Publishers books are available at special quantity discount for sales promotions, or for use in corporate training programs. For more information please write to bulkorders@vibrantpublishers.com

Please email feedback / corrections (technical, grammatical or spelling) to spellerrors@vibrantpublishers.com

To access the complete catalogue of Vibrant Publishers, visit www.vibrantpublishers.com

About the Authors

 **Kalpesh Ashar** is a management consultant and corporate trainer holding an MBA (Dean's Award Winner) from SPJIMR, one of Asia's top business schools, and an Engineering degree with honors in Electronics. He has over 24 years of experience in large organizations and start-ups in Asia, USA, and Europe.

Kalpesh has worked in several project management roles, like Senior Project Manager, Delivery Manager, and Program Manager. He is passionate about writing on management subjects. His techno-business background gives him a unique position to write on management topics that are easy to understand for non-MBA graduates. His books are authored in a simple to understand manner without unnecessary use of management jargon.

James Meersman, who has co-authored this edition of the book (by authoring Chapter 2 - The Accounting Cycle and Chapter 3 - End of Period Accounting Cycle) is an accounting professor holding a PhD from Virginia Tech University and a Masters in Theological Studies from Southwestern Baptist Theological Seminary. He has experience as both a tax consultant and corporate trainer for KPMG, reaching both students and clients across the globe. His experience in corporate setting, ranging from small non-profits to large multinational corporations allows him to delve into the varying roles accounting can play at the organizational level. His simple writing style and hands-on pedagogical approach help encourage critical thinking in both his students and readers alike.

This page is intentionally left blank

What experts say about this book!

This book contains charts, graphics, tables, summary notes and examples related to each chapter and is very informative. It also contains a glossary at the end of the book for students to comprehend the subjects covered. The systematic organization of accounting principles will help students conquer financial accounting.

– Jangho Gil, Assistant Professor of Accounting, Monmouth University

If you are interested in learning about accounting and how to analyze a financial statement, this is a great book to start with. Accounting is an essential skill if you intend to go into business. By doing so, you are protecting yourself against unethical or bad accountants. This book has good insights and gets to the point.

– Xihui Chen, Assistant Professor of Accounting and Finance, Heriot-Watt University

What experts say about this book!

I enjoyed reading Financial Accounting Essentials and I feel that for an overview of the subject matter, this book was well-written. I liked how the book walked the readers through the concepts of accounting.

– Dr Cheryl A Moore, Assistant Professor of Accounting, Mercyhurst University

Regardless of what position you hold in the accounting profession, having a good reference text that will teach you what you need to know and get your questions answered is important. This is an excellent and easy-to-understand text about financial accounting.

– Mike Michelsen, Freelance Writer and Media Professional

Table of Contents

This page is intentionally left blank

Preface

Finance is an area that is important in our everyday life. It is needed at work and at home. Financial Accounting is that part of finance that helps us understand the numbers that our company or business produces. Traditionally, this skill has been confined to those in finance departments or those who studied the subject in school. Over time, we have come to realize that everybody should have financial acumen, as it is a key skill to succeed in personal as well as professional life.

Financial Accounting Essentials You Always Wanted to Know provides that set of bare minimum skills that you need in order to understand financial numbers. It consists of only those key areas that are considered critical. The objective of the book is not to teach you everything in finance, but to equip you with enough information to be more productive and accurate in your decision-making, keeping the financial perspective of your choices in mind.

This page is intentionally left blank

Who can benefit from the book?

This book can be used by anyone who needs to understand financial numbers, like:

- Managers in an organization
- Individuals who need to make investment decisions
- Senior management of an organization

It can also be beneficial for those interested in the field of financial accounting, like:

- Students learning finance as part of their university course
- Anybody else who is interested in learning how to read financial numbers to help in decision-making

How to use this book?

The recommended approach to read this book is to start from the first chapter and go in sequence, even if you are experienced in finance. This will ensure that you get a solid base of the previous chapters that will be needed to understand the later chapters better. There is a lot of financial accounting terminology in each chapter that could be new to you, and understanding it will help you with the later material in the book.

This page is intentionally left blank

Chapter 1

Accounting Systems

In this chapter, we shall look at the fundamentals of financial accounting. These form the pillars for our understanding of the later chapters.

The key learning objectives of this chapter are:

- Understand the different types of accounting systems

- Get introduced to financial statements

An accounting system helps capture and organize information related to business transactions. Depending upon the focus it can be divided into two types:

- Financial Accounting and

- Managerial Accounting.

A Financial Accounting system contains financial statements and disclosures meant for decision makers external to the company. A Managerial Accounting system contains detailed plans and performance reports meant for decision makers within the company.

Figure 1.1

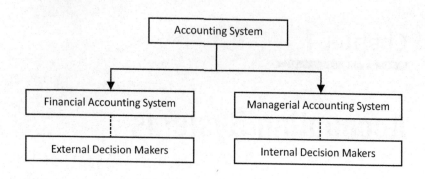

1.1 Financial Accounting Systems

A financial accounting system is a system that serves the dual purpose of keeping track of transaction information and helping organize and evaluate this information primarily meant for external decision makers. The part related to keeping track of information is termed as "Bookkeeping", which is related to recording an activity, like taking a loan, paying a supplier, or receiving a payment. The other part related to organizing information for evaluation is termed as "Financial Statement", which consists of summarised information on the business activities that help in evaluating the health of a business. Bookkeeping is done first and then the captured data is organized and evaluated as part of the Analysis stage.

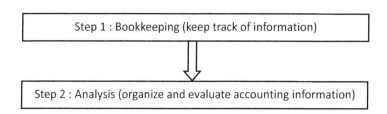

Figure 1.2 Financial Accounting System

Step 1 : Bookkeeping (keep track of information)

Step 2 : Analysis (organize and evaluate accounting information)

1.2 Need for Financial Accounting Systems

Consider the following example. A company buys equipment from another company and pays for it after 10 days. It also produces certain goods and sells 100 units to its customers and receives payment after 30 days. Assume that it also had to raise capital through a bank loan to buy the equipment and produce the goods. If none of these transactions were recorded, it would be impossible to know the amount the company currently owes or needs to receive and therefore, the health status of the company. Hence, bookkeeping (or recording of these transactions) is required by all companies.

Now assume that all transactions are recorded through a bookkeeping system and they are all presented to the external decision makers, like bankers and investors. It would be too difficult for them to wade through so many different transactions to figure out how the company is doing. Hence, financial statements are created from the recorded transactions so as to summarize all transactions under a few well-known heads of accounts. This will enable the external stakeholders to easily read the information and make decisions.

1.3 Financial Statements

There are three main components to a company's financial statements:

a)   Balance Sheet

b)   Income statement (also called Profit and Loss statement)

c)   Statement of Cash Flows

These days, financial statements also contain several mandatory and voluntary disclosures.

Below are simple examples of the three main components.

Balance Sheet

Assets		Liabilities	
Cash	$500.00	Long-term loans	$8,000.00
Land	$4,000.00	Short-term liabilities	$2,000.00
Equipment	$12,000.00		
Other assets	$3,500.00	Equity	
		Owner's investment	$10,000.00
Total	$20,000.00	Total	$20,000.00

A Balance Sheet shows a snapshot of how many resources (assets) a company owns, the company's obligations (liabilities) and the money invested by the owners (equity). As seen above, this is a summarized view that makes it easy to, as opposed to reading each and every transaction of the company. It may also be noted that the total value of assets is exactly equal to the total value of liabilities and equity. The value of assets will always balance against the liabilities and hence the name, Balance Sheet.

Income Statement

Revenues		$15,000
Expenses:		
Cost of raw materials	$5,000	
Salaries	$2,500	
Interest	$500	
Income tax	$800	
Other expenses	$1,000	
Total expenses		$9,800
Net Income		$5,200

An Income Statement (also known as Profit and Loss Statement) reports the revenue earned by the company over a period of time and the expenses incurred. This gives one of the most important measures of a company's health, called Net Income (also called Net Profit). If the expenses are more than revenue, then it results in a loss and the Net Income will be negative (shown in brackets as ($5,200)) as given below.

Revenues		$15,000
Expenses:		
Cost of raw materials	$10,000	
Salaries	$5,000	
Interest	$2,000	
Income tax	$1,500	
Other expenses	$1,700	
Total expenses		$20,200
Net Income		($5,200)

Statement of Cash Flows

Cash from Operating activities:		$5,000.00
Cash used for Investing activities:		
Purchase of property and equipment	($3,500.00)	
Other investments	($500.00)	
		($4,000.00)
Cash from Financing activities:		
New bank loans	$1,500.00	
Repayment of old loans	($500.00)	
Payment of cash dividends	($300.00)	
		$700.00
Net increase in cash during the year		$1,700.00

The Statement of Cash Flows is a report of the amount of cash collected and paid by a company in the given period. Each cash transaction is divided into three types of activities – operating, investing, and financing. It shows the net increase (or net decrease) of cash with the company at the end of the period.

1.4 Purpose of Financial Statements

External parties who need to make decisions about investing in a company, extending a loan to the company or even extending a credit period to the company, do so on the basis of financial statements. The diagram below shows how financial statements are used.

Figure 1.3

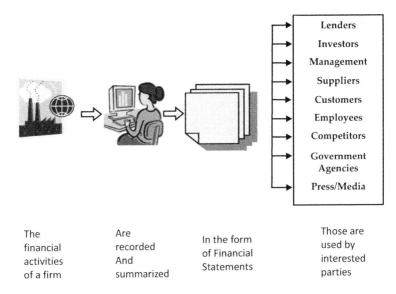

| The financial activities of a firm | Are recorded And summarized | In the form of Financial Statements | Those are used by interested parties |

Below are the main users of financial statements.

a) Lenders

Lenders want to ensure that the company would be in a position to pay interest on a regular basis and the principle at maturity. These are generally banks, individuals, financial institutions and even other companies.

b) Investors

Individual as well as corporate investors invest in a company if they feel that the company can provide attractive returns, based on the risk profile of the company. They can ascertain this by looking at the company's financial statements and assume that the past performance is also representative of the future.

c) Management

Although management has a more detailed view by way of managerial accounting, there are still things in the financial statement that they use, like sales growth, profit margins, cash available, etc.

d) Suppliers

Extending supplier credit is a norm in most industries but suppliers are generally more comfortable extending greater credit periods or greater credit amounts to those companies who they feel would be in a better position to make the payment on the agreed date. They do so by looking at the company's financial statement that provides information about the financial strength and cash available with the company. They also look at the company's past payment record to make a decision.

e) Customers

There are some goods which require a good deal of after-sales support, like aeroplanes. Customers want to know that the aeroplane manufacturer will not go out of business after they buy the plane from them. Financial statements help them gauge the company's financial strength.

f) Employees

Financial statements often determine employees' bonus, pension, health care benefits, etc. A financially strong company is also preferred by employees looking for a secure job.

g) Competitors

Companies often look at the competitor's financial statements to compare their relative performance in terms of revenue, profit, margins etc. This information helps companies to benchmark the best in the industry and devise plans to match or better them.

h) Government Agencies

Federal and state governments, IRS, SEC and other agencies frequently refer to the financial statements of companies to ensure investors' safety and to make policy decisions.

i) Press/Media

Whenever the press wants to report about a company, it can find a significant amount of information in the company's financial statements. Significant events like a large drop in profits, huge losses, and questionable practices are generally predicted with the help of the data present in the financial statements.

1.5 Financial Accounting Standards

In the United States, *FASB* (Financial Accounting Standards Board) sets standards for financial accounting, including financial statements. The accounting rules are described as GAAP (Generally Accepted Accounting Principles).

Apart from FASB, there are other agencies that impact accounting standards and practices as below:

a)   SEC (Securities and Exchange Commission) regulates US stock exchanges and seeks to create a fair information environment in which investors can buy and sell stocks without fear that companies are hiding or manipulating financial data.

b)   AICPA (American Institute of Certified Public Accountants) is a professional organization of certified public accountants (CPAs) in the US. The CPAs provide business advice to companies related to accounting issues.

c)   PCAOB (Public company Accounting Oversight Board) inspects the audit practices of registered audit firms.

d)   IRS (Internal Revenue Service) establishes rules related to how income is to be taxed.

e)   IASB (International Accounting Standards Board) develops common set of worldwide accounting standards.

Solved Examples

1. **Why would the following individuals or groups be interested in a firm's financial statements?**

   a. **Current shareholders of the firm**

   b. **Creditors of the firm**

   c. **Management of the firm**

Solution:

   a. **Current shareholders of the firm**

   The current shareholders of the firm would look at the financial statements for 3 reasons – to decide if the stock is worth holding or selling, whether additional investment can be made in the company, and to ensure that the management is keeping shareholder interests in mind while making decisions. The last part has become exceedingly important now with several individuals and groups filing class action lawsuits on firms.

   b. **Creditors of the firm**

   Individuals or groups would extend credit to a firm on the basis of the strength of their financial statements. This will help them decide on the amount of risk involved in extending credit and accordingly decide on the quantum and period of the credit.

c. **Management of the firm**

The management might decide targets based on the company's financial statements. These could be in the form of profit growth percentage, sales growth percentage, decrease in the overhead costs, etc.

2. **Comment on the following balance sheet of a firm.**

Assets		Liabilities	
Cash	$5,000.00	Long-term loans	$15,000.00
Land	$20,000.00	Short-term liabilities	$10,000.00
Equipment	$10,000.00		
Other assets	$1,000.00	Equity	
		Owner's investment	$10,000.00
Total	$36,000.00	Total	$35,000.00

Solution:

The Balance Sheet above is incorrect as the Total Assets are not the same as Total Liabilities and Equity. A Balance Sheet should have an exact match between these two totals.

Practice Exercise

1. Comment on the income statement below.

Revenues		$5,000.00
Expenses:		
Cost of raw materials	$3,000.00	
Salaries	$2,000.00	
Interest	$1,000.00	
Income tax	$ -	
Total expenses		$6,000.00
Net Income		($1,000.00)

2. In what way would the following individuals or groups be interested in a firm's financial statements?

   a. Prospective shareholders of the firm

   b. SEC (Securities and Exchange Commission)

   c. Firm's major labor union

Solutions to the above questions can be downloaded from the **Online Resources** *section of this book on* **www.vibrantpublishers.com**

Chapter Summary

◆ Accounting Systems can be divided into Financial Accounting System and Managerial Accounting System, used by external decision makers and internal decision makers respectively.

◆ Financial Accounting Systems consist of two activities: bookkeeping and analysis. Bookkeeping refers to keeping a record of all financial transactions over a period of time. Analysis refers to organizing this information into Financial Statements, which are used to analyse the health of the company and to make decisions.

◆ Financial Statements consist of three major parts – Balance Sheet, Income Statement (also called Profit & Loss Statement), and the Statement of Cash Flows. Notes to Financial Statements provide more details about some of the headings in these major parts.

◆ A Balance Sheet shows a snapshot of how many resources (assets) a company owns, the company's obligations (liabilities) and the money invested by the owners (equity).

◆ An Income Statement (also known as Profit & Loss Statement) reports the revenue earned by the company over a period of time and the expenses incurred.

◆ The Statement of Cash Flows reports the amount of cash collected and paid by the company in the given period.

◆ Parties who are generally interested in the financial statements are lenders, investors, management, suppliers, customers, employees, competitors, government agencies, and press/media.

◆ Financial Statements are to be reported as per the applicable accounting practices and standards, which could vary from region to region.

This page is intentionally left blank

Chapter 2

The Accounting Cycle

Chapter two introduces the Accounting Cycle through the lens of measuring economic activity. While the general term "accounting" can mean many things, this chapter reveals the most basic principles of how accounting works. In knowing these concepts, one can then begin to build on this knowledge through various financial statements and how transactions impact those statements.

Key learning objectives should include the reader's understanding of the following:

- Measuring economic activities
- Assets and examples of these accounts
- Liabilities and examples of these accounts
- Stockholders' equity and examples of these accounts
- Increasing accounts
- Decreasing accounts

2.1 Measuring Economic Activities

The primary purpose of the accounting cycle is to limit the measurement of the economic activities of a company to a standardized amount of time. While many companies operate on a calendar year basis (e.g. January 1 – December 31), some companies operate on what is known as a fiscal year, meaning that their operating cycle is captured by non-standard dates (e.g. February 1 – January 31, June 1 – May 31, etc.). Note that the unit of measurement is still one full year and is broken up among 12 months and 4 quarters. In context of the primary functions of accounting (measure economic activities and communicate those results), the accounting cycle adds consistency to reporting and allows individuals to compare performance across years and across companies. In order to start this process, one needs to understand the definition of both internal and external transactions.

External transactions can be defined as economic activities between a company and a separate entity, while internal transactions are economic activities within a company that do not involve a separate entity. Both types of transactions occur very frequently within a company, and many times both types of transactions may relate to a singular event. These transactions are measured and recorded based on how they impact what is called the accounting equation. The accounting equation is a simple representation that reflects all of a company's resources and who has claims to those resources:

Assets = Liabilities + Stock Holders' Equity

In the equation above, the Assets refer to all resources to which the company has access. These resources are defined as assets because they can be used to generate future revenue. Liabilities are obligations a company has to use assets in the future. The simplest example of this would be a bank loan. While a company who takes a loan out now has more cash, they will ultimately have to pay that money back to the bank (i.e. they are obligated to use future cash to satisfy the bank loan). Stock holders' equity reveals how much money has been given to the company by way of investors, how much profit the company has earned over the course of its life, and how much money has been given back to investors in the form of dividends. While there are only three components to the accounting equation, each component is made of up various accounts. These accounts are what change with each transaction that a company undertakes, whether it be internal or external. It is important to note that the accounting equation is always in balance. This also implies that every economic transaction affects at least two accounts.

2.2 Increasing and Decreasing Accounts

While the accounting equation is always in balance, the accounts within the accounting equation must also be adjusted with every transaction that occurs. Some common accounts that are used within most public companies are items like cash, accounts receivable, accounts payable, common stock, revenue, costs of goods sold, and inventory. While there are dozens of different accounts that can be impacted with any given transaction, these are just a few of the more common ones. Whenever an economic transaction occurs, one must understand how that transaction impacts the accounting equation. For instance, the cash that was borrowed in the previous example, two types of activities are occurring: (1) cash is being received by the company from the bank, and (2) a loan (or note payable) is being added to the company by the bank. So the resources (assets) of the company are increasing, but the obligations of the company to pay that money back to the bank (liabilities) are also increasing. So both assets and liabilities are increasing by the same amount, resulting in the accounting equation being balanced. Note that in this scenario, the stockholders' equity was not impacted. The company then uses those resources (assets), in this case cash, to generate revenue by spending the money on various things (advertising, inventory, land, utilities, etc.). Spending this money is considered another transaction, and will also impact the accounting equation, while still resulting in a balanced accounting equation.

Now that we understand why the accounting equation is impacted by transactions, we must also discuss how it is impacted. In the previous example, both cash and notes payable were increasing, but how does one increase both of these accounts? This is done by posting a journal entry. A journal entry is a chronological record of all economic transactions. Depending on the type, each account will increase by recording that amount on either the left or the right side of the journal entry. It is important to note the following points:

1. **Asset and expense accounts increase by recording an amount on the left side of the journal entry and decrease by recording the amount on the right side of the journal entry.**

2. **Liability and Stockholders' equity accounts increase by recording an amount on the right side of the journal entry**

and decrease by recording the amount on the left side of the journal entry.

Consider the following journal entry from our previous example:

Cash	$XX	
Notes Payable		$XX

In this example, both accounts were increasing. Cash (an asset) increases with a left entry (see above), while Notes Payable (a liability) increases with a right entry (see above). Since both items were increasing as a result of the transaction, both were reflected as increasing through their appropriate journal entries. Note that the left column and the right column balance. While this is just one transaction, in reality, a company would have hundreds or even thousands of these types of left/right entries, and in every case, the left side and right side would balance (just like in the accounting equation). It is also important to note that the perspective you should be taking with this exercise is always from the company. If you were an accountant for the bank, who was giving out the loan, then your journal entry would look different. Because we are taking the perspective of the company, our journal entry looks like the illustration above.

Consider the following five journal entry examples for an auto mechanic shop:

1. Received a cash loan from a bank of $400,000.

2. Used the cash from the bank loan to purchase a piece of land for $100,000.

3. Used the cash from the bank loan to build a new building for $300,000.

4. Completed auto services for customers in current month of $40,000 cash.

5. Paid employees' salaries for the current month of $5,000 cash.

Journal Entries

Date	Account Name	Left	Right	Balance
(1)	Cash	$400,000		
(1)	Notes Payable		$400,000	
(2)	Land	$100,000		
(2)	Cash		$100,000	
(3)	Building	$300,000		
(3)	Cash		$300,000	
(4)	Cash	$40,000		
(4)	Service Revenue		$40,000	
(5)	Salaries Expense	$5,000		
(5)	Cash		$5,000	

After a general overview of the accounting equation and journal entries have been discussed, it is also relevant to define the General Ledger. The General Ledger (GL), is a single location housing all account types and transaction information related to each account. This means that when a journal entry is recorded (see previous illustration above), that same information is then posted to those specific account balances within the GL:

General Ledger

Cash

Date	Description	Left	Right	Balance
(1)	Cash from loan	$400,000		$400,000
(2)	Land Purchase		$100,000	$300,000
(3)	Building Purchase		$300,000	$ -
(4)	Current month services	$40,000		$40,000
(5)	Current month salaries		$5000	$35,000

Note Payable

Date	Description	Left	Right	Balance
(1)	Loan from bank		$400,000	$400,000

Land

Date	Description	Left	Right	Balance
(2)	Land Purchase	$100,000		$100,000

Building

Date	Description	Left	Right	Balance
(3)	Building Purchase	$300,000		$300,000

Service Revenue

Date	Description	Left	Right	Balance
(4)	Current month services		$40,000	$40,000

Salaries Expense

Date	Description	Left	Right	Balance
(5)	Current month salaries	$5000		$5000

This is an important component of the accounting cycle because it reveals the most current balance of each account at any given moment, allowing management to make the most appropriate decisions.

Once the accounting cycle is over, the ending balances from the GL can be combined into what is called the pre-closing trial balance. The pre-closing trial balance provides a summary of every account balance at the end of the period before the closing process. Every account within the GL will have either a left balance or a right balance. After considering the accounting equation, journal entries, the general ledger, and the trial balance, the accounting cycle concludes with the closing process, which will be covered in chapter 3.

Solved Examples

1. **Which of the following parties should be interested in a public firm's economic activity and why?**

   a. Firm employees

   b. Regulatory bodies

   c. Firm shareholders

   d. Institutional investors who have not yet invested in the company

Solution:

They should all be considered parties interested in a firm's economic activity.

a. **Firm employees:** The activity of a firm is of great interest to the firm's employees because their continued employment opportunities rely on the economic activity of their employer.

b. **Regulatory bodies:** Regulatory bodies find meaning in the economic activity of a firm, because this activity impacts the economy as a whole. Regulatory bodies are tasked with governing the economic activity of their jurisdiction, including that of the public firm in question.

c. **Firm shareholders:** Firm shareholders need to understand the economic activity of the firm in which they are invested in order to make a future decision about their investment in the firm (e.g. buy more stock, sell stock, hold their currently owned stock, etc.).

d. Institutional investors not yet invested in the company: These potential investors also need know about the economic activity of a public firm in order to understand whether investing in the firm is a good investment.

Practice Exercise

1. Give a journal entry and update the general ledger for the following five transactions involving a new car taxi service:

   a. Obtain a $25,000 loan from a community bank.

   b. Spend $25,000 cash for a new taxi vehicle.

   c. Earn $3,000 cash transporting customers in the current month.

   d. Spend $1,000 cash for fuel in the current month.

   e. Spend $500 cash on repairs for the taxi vehicle.

	Journal Entries			
Date	Account Name	Left	Right	Balance
(1)				
(1)				
(2)				
(2)				
(3)				
(3)				
(4)				
(4)				
(5)				
(5)				

General Ledger

Cash

Date	Description	Left	Right	Balance

Note Payable

Date	Description	Left	Right	Balance

Vehicle

Date	Description	Left	Right	Balance

Fuel Expense

Date	Description	Left	Right	Balance

Service Revenue

Date	Description	Left	Right	Balance

Repair Expense				
Date	Description	Left	Right	Balance

Discussion Questions

1. What stuck out to you the most in this chapter?

2. Was there anything in this chapter that you already knew?

3. Are there ways you think this chapter might apply to future or past chapters within this book?

4. Are there ways you think this chapter might apply to other courses you have taken or other books you have read?

5. Are there any real-world examples you can think of that apply the concepts laid out in this chapter?

6. Find the financial statements of a public company (Yahoo finance should be an appropriate resource for this) and answer the following questions.

   a) Are there any terms in the financial statements that you also see in this chapter?

   b) Give some examples of assets found in your company's financial statements.

   c) Give some examples of liabilities found in your company's financial statements.

   d) Give some examples of stockholders' equity line items found in your company's financial statements.

Chapter Summary

◆ The accounting cycle is an important component for any organization looking to communicate its financial management to external parties.

◆ The primary purpose of this cycle is to limit the measurement of the economic activities of a company to a standardized amount of time. This is usually done by capturing both external and internal transactions.

◆ External transactions can be defined as economic activities between a company and a separate entity, while internal transactions are economic activities within a company that do not involve a separate entity.

◆ Capturing these activities is fulfilled through increasing and decreasing accounts through journal entries which are summarized in the general ledger.

This page is intentionally left blank

Chapter 3

End of Period Accounting Cycle

Chapter three introduces the process of ending the accounting cycle period. While the accounting cycle (chapter two) bears much weight in terms of its role in financial accounting, the end of the period must be fully complete before the financial statements can be developed. As such, understanding how this period ends and the associated requirements it creates is crucial towards fully understanding financial accounting.

Key learnings from this chapter include the reader's understanding of the following:

- Cash accounting

- Accrual accounting

- Accrued revenue

- Incurred expense

- Financial statements

- Statement of stockholders' equity

- Income statement

- Balance sheet

3.1 Cash vs. Accrual Accounting

Now that a brief overview of the accounting cycle has been discussed, it is important to understand various accounting methods before continuing on to the closing of the accounting cycle. Chapter Two took the perspective of what is known as the "Accrual" method. This method, which is consistent with GAAP and is the method adopted by all public corporations, aims to measure the economic transactions that have taken place within a company. This method may seem counterintuitive at first, as the economics of a transaction sometimes do not match the actual cash that exchanges hands. Before diving further into accrual accounting, let us look at the "Cash" method in detail..

Cash accounting is very simple. This method can largely be summed with the following rules:

1. **A journal entry in the books of accounts is required only when cash has exchanged hands.**

2. **Cash received is ALWAYS booked as revenue, regardless of where it is derived from.**

3. **Cash given is ALWAYS booked as an expense, regardless of to whom the cash is given.**

This may seem simple at first, but let's consider two extreme examples to drive the point:

a) **Company A receives a $1,000 cash loan from a bank.**

b) **Company B receives $1,000 cash for work performed in the current period.**

Under cash accounting, BOTH companies would recognize $1,000 of revenue because they both received cash of $1,000. Even though Company A will have to pay the loan back, that cash is treated as revenue under the cash accounting rules. Cash accounting is not consistent with GAAP, meaning that public companies are not able to use this method. That being said, this method is much easier to master, so it is more commonly used by smaller companies or local businesses.

3.2 Accruing Revenues and Incurring Expenses

Back to accrual accounting, an economic approach is more appropriate to use because it maximizes faithful representation of the financial statements. Why is this method more faithfully representative? Consider this example; imagine a company you are considering to invest in published profits that are twice as high as last year's performance. You would initially be very pleased and would likely seek to invest in this company, maybe even more than what you were originally seeking to invest. Now consider the possibility that the company did not earn all of that revenue (i.e. as was done by Company B in example (b) above). Instead, the company took out a hefty loan from a bank in order to appear to be more profitable (i.e. as was done by Company A in example (a) above). Under the cash method, this company would be accounting for their revenue correctly, but their revenue performance is not representative of what actually occurred throughout the year. This is where accrual accounting comes in.

For the purposes of this book, consider the following differentiating features of accrual accounting:

1. **Revenue is ONLY booked when it has been earned, regardless of whether the cash has been received.**

2. **Expenses are ONLY booked when they have been incurred, regardless of whether the payment has been made.**

Consider the same examples that were mentioned above. Company A would not book any revenue, because they did not earn any of the cash. In contrast Company B would still book revenue because they did the work to earn the revenue. Notice that sometimes work can be completed without receiving any cash immediately. Regardless, revenue should still be book, even if the cash has yet to be received.

Let's consider an example regarding expenses. Company C prepaid their rent in advance for 12 months on January 1, of $6,000 ($500 per month). Company C's journal entry on January 1 will look like the following:

Prepaid Rent (Asset)	$6,000	
Cash (Asset)		$6,000

Company D, in a similar building with similar rental terms, did not pay anything in advance. They will make no journal entry because they paid no cash and incurred no expense. At the end of the first month, BOTH companies will book a rental expense of $500. However, Company D will have to pay cash to the landlord after incurring the expense, while Company C has already paid for the rent (in advance). So while both companies incurred the same rent at the same time, one company paid the cash earlier than the other. See the example journal entries for each company below:

Company C

Rent Expense (Expense)	$500	
Prepaid Rent (Asset)		$500
Company D		
Rent Expense (Expense)	$500	
Cash (Asset)		$500

3.3 Financial Statement Reporting

Now that a brief summary of accrual and cash accounting has been given, it is important to understand the practical application of accrual accounting in the real world. The two primary goals of accounting is to measure both economic activity and communicate that activity to interested parties. Since the measuring aspect of accounting has been discussed, the communication aspect can now be revealed. The primary way to communicate accounting information to the public is through the following four financial statements:

a) Income Statement

b) Balance Sheet

c) Statement of Cash Flows

d) Statement of Stockholders Equity

These statements disclose various aspects of the financial performance of a company in different ways. While this section is only meant to be a primer, it is important to have a rudimentary understanding of each of the four financial statements.

The income statement is a measure of a company's profit. While this statement is composed of many layers of earnings, the most simple income statement formula is the following: REVENUE – EXPENSES = NET INCOME. In a real-world application, a company has many forms of both revenues and expenses. For instance, some companies have costs of goods sold, if they sold inventory, while some companies may have numerous types of revenue if they offer both inventory and services.

The Balance Sheet is a snapshot of the resources of a company and who has claims to those resources in the current period. This definition is similar to the accounting equation. The simple formula for the balance sheet is the following: ASSETS = LIABILTIES + STOCKHOLDER'S EQUITY. This formula can be further broken down into additional components, but this should serve as an adequate summary of the balance sheet.

The Statement of Cash Flows seeks to reveal the cash status of a company. This part of the financial statement is very important, as it shows how the capacity of a company to accomplish tasks like take on new projects, perform research and development, pay current debts, or issue dividends. The formula for the statement of cash flows is summarized by the cash inflows and outflows of the following categories: OPERATING ACTIVITIES + INVESTING ACTIVITIES + FINANCING ACTIVITIES. Operating activities reflect the daily operations of the company; investing activities reflects cash spent or earned on items that are long-term (over one year) in nature; financing activities reflect activities that help finance the company (e.g. issuing common stock, etc.).

The Statement of Stockholders' Equity the capital structure of the company and who has ownership interests in it. This is where investors will look to see how many dividends (or payments back to shareholders) were issued in the current period. The simple formula for this financial statement is the following: COMMON STOCK + RETAINED EARNINGS (e.g. Net Income – Dividends). Common stock is usually only issued at the inception of a company, though more common stock and other types of stock can be issued later on.

Solved Examples

1. **Why is ending the accounting cycle important? What factors would impact the decision to select cash versus accrual accounting?**

Solution:

Ending the accounting cycle is an important component of the overall accounting cycle because it helps clearly establish the boundaries of economic activity within a given time frame of a firm. This component allows stakeholders to understand the financial performance of a firm and compare the performance to other firms.

There are a lot of factors that go into deciding between cash versus accrual accounting. However, larger public corporations are generally required to implement accrual accounting. While cash accounting is a somewhat easier method of accounting, it does not appropriately reflect the economics of financial transactions between firms. Thus, cash accounting is more prevalent in smaller businesses without regulatory requirements.

Practice Exercise

1. How much net income would Company A report with the following information:

    a. Cash $100

    b. Revenue $850

    c. Rent Expense $300

    d. Salaries Expense $300

    e. Prepaid Rent $1,200

    Give a journal entry using both the "Cash" and "Accrual" accounting methods for the following transactions:

    i. Company E receives a $3,000 cash loan from a bank.

    ii. Company E incurred $1,000 of rent in the current month. They did not prepay rent.

    iii. Company F receives $4,000 cash for work performed in the current period.

    iv. Company F incurred $2,000 of rent in the current month. They already prepaid $24,000 of rent in the beginning of the month.

CASH METHOD

Journal Entries

Date	Account Name	Left	Right	Cash Balance
(1)				
(1)				
(2)				
(2)				
(3)				
(3)				
(4)				
(4)				

ACCURAL METHOD

Journal Entries

Date	Account Name	Left	Right	Cash Balance
(1)				
(1)				
(2)				
(2)				
(3)				
(3)				
(4)				
(4)				

Solutions to the above questions can be downloaded from the **Online Resources** *section of this book on*
www.vibrantpublishers.com

Discussion Questions

1. What stuck out to you the most in this chapter?

2. Was there anything in this chapter that you already knew?

3. Are there ways you think this chapter might apply to future or past chapters within this book?

4. Are there ways you think this chapter might apply to other courses you have taken or other books you have read?

5. Are there any real-world examples you can think of that apply the concepts laid out in this chapter?

6. Use the financial statements of the same public company used in the previous chapter and answer the following questions.

   a) Are there any terms in the financial statements that you also see in this chapter?

   b) Can you find any examples of accrued revenues? Which financial statement are these examples found?

   c) Can you find any examples of incurred expenses? Which financial statement are these examples found?

   d) Try to locate the key items that link the four financial statements together.

Chapter Summary

◆ Ending the accounting cycle is a crucial component of any organization's accounting system. Once the regular activity of a business concludes, the end of period accounting cycle helps to summarize the economic activity of that business in order to communicate the results to external parties.

◆ There are two types of accounting systems (cash and accrual), both of which have their strengths and weaknesses. While cash accounting is an easier approach, accrual accounting does a better job of reflecting the economic transaction of a company. These transactions are reflected in what is known as the financial statement: income statement, balance sheet, statement of cash flows, and the statement of stockholders equity.

Chapter 4

Overview of Financial Statements

This chapter covers the various parts of a financial statement.

The key learning objectives of this chapter are:

- Introduction to balance sheet
- Introduction to income statement
- Introduction to the statement of cash flows

As mentioned in the previous section, financial statements are made up of three primary items:

a) Balance Sheet,

b) Income Statement, and

c) Statement of Cash Flows.

In the following sections we will describe what falls under each of these items and their significance.

4.1 Balance Sheet

A balance sheet is a snapshot of a company's source and application of funds on any given date. Companies prepare a balance sheet every quarter and it reflects the company's state on the last day of the quarter.

There are three items that go into a balance sheet:

a) Assets,

b) Liabilities, and

c) Owners' Equity (also called Stockholders' Equity).

Figure 4.1

ASSETS	LIABILITIES
	OWNERS' EQUITY
Total Assets =	Total Liabilities and Owners' Equity

Assets

These are the economic resources of a firm that provide probable future economic benefits due to ownership or control as a result of past transactions or events. Each part of this definition is important. Firstly, "probable benefit" points to a future benefit that ownership of the asset could fetch, like higher sales due to ownership of a machine or new business due to ownership of an office building. Secondly, asset is something that should provide "future economic benefit". This makes anything you own an asset only if it is expected to bring a benefit in future, irrespective of past benefits. Finally, "ownership or control as a result of past transactions or events" means that the company should have either ownership or control over the asset, to reap the benefit, and it will always be due to a past transaction, like buying a building or acquiring equipment.

Following are some examples of Assets:

a) Cash

b) Accounts Receivable

c) Inventory

d) Prepaid expenses

e) Land

f) Buildings

g) Fixtures and equipment

h) Marketable securities

i) Goodwill (this asset has to be specifically bought in an economic transaction to be recognized as an asset)

Assets appear either on the left-hand side of the balance sheet (in side-by-side format) or at the top (in columnar format). We shall discuss both formats later.

Liabilities

These are obligations of an economic nature for a firm that might need a future sacrifice of economic benefits that are a result of current obligations, to give away assets or to provide services to others in the future due to past transactions or events. These are the exact opposite of assets. The "probable future sacrifices" hint towards a payment of some kind that the company would need to make in future, like payment to creditors, bank, suppliers etc. The part about "transfer assets or provide services" refer to an obligation to give up an asset or provide a service, both of which may not be cash transactions but would still consume the company's resources. For example, if a company has sold equipment with a one year warranty, it is obligated to provide service if a fault is detected. This becomes the company's liability. Like assets, a liability also occurs due to "past transactions or events".

Below are some examples of Liabilities:

   a) Short-term loans payable

   b) Accounts payable

   c) Accrued salaries and wages

   d) Long-term notes and debentures

   e) Long-term loans payable

Liabilities appear either on the right-hand side of the balance sheet (in side-by-side format) or at the bottom (in columnar format).

Owners' Equity (Stockholders' Equity)

This is the component that belongs to the owners of the company and includes shareholders. As the company does its business, it either generates profits or incurs losses. Owners' equity increases if it makes profit. If it makes losses, owners' equity reduces. Similarly, if the proprietor withdraws money from the company or the company buys back its own shares, then owners' equity reduces. We will see more details about how transactions affect owners' equity in later chapters.

The three predominant components of owners' equity are Paid-in Capital, Retained Earnings and Treasury Stock. These are described below:

Paid-in Capital

When owners of a company invest cash or other assets in the business, they receive shares of stock in exchange. This gets added to paid-in capital. For example, if a company goes for an IPO (Initial Public Offering) to raise $100 million, then once the IPO is over, its paid-in capital would increase by $100 million provided it is able to get full subscription of its new stocks.

It is important to note that when shares are sold in the stock exchange (secondary market), that transaction does not affect owners' equity as it is a market transaction between two investors. The company does not receive anything other than the initial investment when the stock was issued.

Retained Earnings

This is generally expected to be the largest component of the owners' equity for profitable companies as it reflects the accumulated profits of the company. Each year the company reports either profit or loss in its financial statements. These get added to or subtracted from the retained earnings in the balance sheet. Consider an example where a company starts operations this year and makes a profit of $10,000 this year (this will be shown in the Net Income of the Income Statement). Assuming that the company does not have to pay any dividends, $10,000 will reflect in the Retained Earnings of the Balance Sheet at the end of this year. Now if the company makes a profit of $40,000 next year and, once again, does not pay out any dividend, the Retained Earnings would become $50,000 at the end of the second year. The sheet below shows this condition.

Income Statement	Year 1	Year 2
Revenues	$50,000	$250,000
Expenses	$40,000	$200,000
Net Income	$10,000	$50,000
Balance Sheet	Year 1	Year 2
Assets	-	-
Liabilities	-	-
Stockholders' Equity	-	-
Paid-in Capital	-	-
Retained Earnings	$10,000 ⟶	$60,000

Treasury Stock

Several times highly profitable companies buyback their own shares from the market. This serves two purposes. It is a way of distributing profits to shareholders and also sending positive signals to the market about the company's future. When the company performs a buyback, the treasury stock goes up and that amount gets subtracted from the total owners' equity. Hence, greater the treasury stock, lower the owners' equity.

Below is an example.

Number of shares issued (also called outstanding): 10,000

Face value of each share: $1

Hence, Paid-in Capital = $10,000

The Balance Sheet looks like this:

Assets	$10,000
Total Assets	$10,000
Liabilities	$0
Stockholders' Equity	-
Paid-in Capital	$10,000
Treasury Stock	$0
Total Liabilities and Equity	$10,000

Now, let's say that the company decides to buyback $5,000 worth of shares. This will increase the Treasury stock as below. Any increase in Treasury stock is subtracted from the Total Equity as the company has paid money to buy the shares.

Assets	$5,000
Total Assets	$5,000
Liabilities	$0
Stockholders' Equity	-
Paid-in Capital	$10,000
Treasury Stock	($5,000)
Total Liabilities and Equity	$5,000

It may also be noted that the Assets are also reduced by the same amount, as Cash, an asset, was used to buyback the shares. This reduces the Total Assets by the same amount as the Treasury Stock.

Balance Sheet Formats

As stated earlier, a Balance Sheet has two formats – side-by-side and columnar. The columnar format has the advantage of being able to input figures from the previous year for comparison and therefore is a preferred format in most cases. The diagrams below show both the formats.

Side-by-Side Format

Assets		Liabilities	
Cash	$500.00	Short-term loans	$200.00
Land	$4,000.00	Bonds	$300.00
		Stockholders' Equity	
		Paid-up capital	$100.00
		Retained earnings	$ 300.00
Total Assets	$900.00	Total Liabilities and Stockholders' Equity	$900.00

Columnar Format

Assets	2021	2020
Cash	$500.00	$400.00
Land	$400.00	$300.00
Total Assets	$900.00	$700.00

Liabilities and Stockholders' Equity	2021	2020
Short-term loans	$200.00	$150.00
Bonds	$300.00	$300.00
Total Liabilities	$500.00	$450.00
Paid-up capital	$100.00	$50.00
Retained earnings	$300.00	$200.00
Total Stockholders' Equity	$400.00	$250.00
Total Liabilities and Stockholders' Equity	$900.00	$700.00

The Accounting Equation

As we saw in the previous section, there is a relation between Assets and Liabilities and Stockholders' Equity. This forms the accounting equation given below.

$$Assets = Liabilities + Stockholders'\ Equity$$

OR

$$A = L + E$$

The above relation is always true for any company as assets can be created either through greater liabilities or more investment from stockholders/owners.

Concepts and Conventions

The Balance Sheet is based on certain concepts.

Entity Concept

Every corporation is treated as a separate entity, different from other corporations and also different from its owners or shareholders. This means that personal finances have to be kept separate from the corporation's finances. For example, if the proprietor of a company buys a house, it does not reflect on the financial statement of the company he owns. It is his personal asset. Similarly, if his company buys an office, it will have no effect on the proprietor's personal financial statements, as this asset will be shown on the company's balance sheet.

Historical Costs Convention

All assets in the balance sheet are valued at the price at which they were acquired. For example, land, building and equipment are listed at their buying price, irrespective of their current price. Similarly, the liabilities are also recorded according to their historical costs. Let's say that a company bought a piece of land for $500,000 in the year 2000. The Balance sheet would show it as an asset worth $50,000. Even though the land value appreciates to $1,000,000 in the year 2020, the company's Balance sheet will show it to be worth $500,000. This means that the company does not carry out valuation of its assets every year. All assets are shown as per their original cost price.

Going Concern

Every balance sheet is prepared on the basis of an assumption that the company will continue to do its business in the future. Without this assumption, the company would need to re-assess the value of all its assets as if it were going out of business, and the balance sheet would look very different. For example, the company could be holding inventory bought at $10,000 but the resale value of that inventory is only $1,000. The company would show the inventory worth $10,000 in its Balance sheet with the assumption that it will continue to do business and use the inventory; it is not going out of business and, hence, does not need to sell its assets right now. It is not liquidating its assets. Without this assumption, the company would need to carry out a revaluation of its assets every quarter/year and that would not be correct as the company is actually not planning to sell them but use them for business purposes.

4.2 Income Statement

An income statement is a statement of the company's revenues and expenses over a period of time –a month, a quarter, a half-year or a year. The company's revenue is termed as the "top line" whereas its net income is termed as "bottom line". Both these items are there on the income statement. It may be noted that the Income Statement contains values that are, to a large extent, "estimates" and may not be "real". All "real" values are present in the statement of cash flows.

The diagram below shows an Income Statement:

Figure 4.2

REVENUES:	$500
EXPENSES:	$300
NET INCOME:	$200

Revenues

Every company operates with the objective of generating money from its business. It achieves this by selling products or services and in doing so generates Revenue. Revenue can take many forms, like sales, licensing, franchising, renting, investing, etc. Companies generally use two different heads for revenue. One is for the Sales that form the core business of the company and other is the "Other revenue" that comes from other sources, like interest incomes, rent, etc.

Expenses

Every company needs to spend money while doing business and generating revenues. This is called Expense and it can taken on various forms. It can be directly on the product being sold and is called "Cost of Goods Sold". It can contain a list of operating overheads and selling and marketing expenses which are termed as "Selling, General, and Administrative Expenses". Then there are other expenses like Interest expense and Income tax expense.

Gains and Losses

Sometimes companies may have gains or losses in activities which are not considered as core business activities, like foreign exchange gain/loss or gain/loss from holdings in other companies. Similarly, if a grocery store sells a pickup truck at a profit, it does not reflect in Sales as it is not a gain from its normal business. It is included under the heading Gains and Losses.

Net Income

This is the difference between the revenues and expenses. If it is negative then there is a net loss. If a company has a net income then it gets added to the retained earnings in the balance sheet after removing any cash dividends. Similarly, a net loss reduces the retained earnings in the balance sheet.

Dividends

Companies pay out cash dividends to their shareholders. This is a way of sharing profits. However, Dividends do not appear on the Income Statement. They are added after the Income Statement ends (after Net Income). The remaining portion of the Net Income gets added to the Retained Earnings of the Balance Sheet.

Concepts and Conventions

The Income Statement is based on certain concepts and conventions as below:

Time Period Concept

An income statement shows the revenues, expenses and net income over a period of time as against the balance sheet, which shows assets, liabilities and stockholders' equity at a particular point of time. Most companies create an income statement at least quarterly. This requires judgment on the part of the company's accountants to report partially completed transactions. For example, the company's financial statements that are published every quarter will show a period against the Income Statement, whereas, the Balance Sheet will be "as of" a certain date as shown below.

Income Statement from Jan 1, 2021 to Mar 31, 2021

Balance Sheet as on Mar 31, 2021

Revenue Recognition

There will be transactions that continue for long, starting from order generation to receiving the payment. But this period could see several income statements being created. In such a case it becomes difficult to decide whether the revenue for that transaction should be included (recognized) in the income statement. The following two criteria are used to determine when to recognize revenue:

a) Before recognizing revenue, the promised work must be done, meaning that the goods should have been delivered or the service must have been provided.

b) Before recognizing revenue, cash must have been collected, or, at least, collection must be reasonably assured.

4.3 Statement of Cash Flows

This is the only statement that contains "real" values of money spent or collected. The only time an entry comes on this statement is when money either goes out from or comes into the account of the organization. The cash items on this statement are divided into three main activities – operating, investing and financing.

The diagram below shows a Statement of Cash Flows.

Figure 4.3

Net cash provided by Operating activities:	$500
Net cash used in Investing activities:	($300)
Net cash provided by Financing activities:	$100
Increase in Cash during the year:	$500 - $300 + $100 = $300

Operating Activities

All the regular business activities of the business that either use or bring in cash are shown under Cash flow from Operating activities. There would be several entries that would either generate or consume cash and finally provide "Net Cash provided by Operating activities". If this value is negative then the company is utilizing more cash than it is generating from its normal business activities.

Investing Activities

When a company buys manufacturing equipment, land or building which becomes an asset to help it run its regular business, all these activities are called investing activities. Similarly, sale of land will also be an investing activity that brings in cash. All the inflow and outflow of cash is then netted under the head "Net cash used in Investing activities". This implies that a company is expected to have a net cash outflow (a negative value) for this head. This is generally true as these investments add to the company's assets for future benefits.

Financing Activities

The company borrows money from various sources and also returns them at maturity. All these activities are called financing activities and the head "Net cash provided by Financing activities" shows whether the company has borrowed more than it has returned over the period of time (positive net means the company has borrowed more than it has returned).

In the following example, the company has made cash from operating activities, has a net investment in assets and is also a net borrower over the specified period of time. It can be said that this company is generating cash from its operations and is utilizing a large part of that in investing in assets. Finally, the excess cash from operations and financing increases the cash available with the company (an asset), as seen from "Net increase in cash during the year".

Net cash provided by Operating activities		$5,000.00
Investing activities:		
Purchase of property and equipment	($3,500.00)	
Other investments	($500.00)	
Net Cash used in Investing activities		($4,000.00)
Financing activities:		
New bank loans	$1,500.00	
Repayment of old loans	($500.00)	
Payment of cash dividends	($300.00)	
Net cash provided by Financing activities		$700.00
Net increase in cash during the year		$1,700.00

4.4 Notes to the Financial Statements

Apart from the three main parts of the financial statements, Balance sheet, Income statement and Statement of Cash Flows, there are a few additional sections. These can be categorized under four general heads as below:

Summary of Significant Accounting Policies

This section documents various assumptions, estimates and judgments made in creating the financial statement.

Additional Information about Summary Totals

Companies summarize several heads under a single summary to make the financial statement readable. However, each of these summaries could have several items under them which give detailed information to the reader. For example, a single summary called Long-term Loans could be broken up into several loans, debentures, bonds with different maturities and amounts.

Disclosure Information Not Recognized

Revenue recognition concept is applied while compiling the financial statement. But in some cases, like liabilities that could arise due to a lawsuit revenue cannot be recognized. Such items are included in this section. These are also called contingent liabilities.

Supplementary Information

These include mandatory information required by FASB and SEC in all financial statements.

4.5 Miscellaneous Accounting Concepts and Conventions

Apart from the concepts and conventions that are applied separately to the Balance Sheet and Income Statement, there are certain other concepts and conventions that are applicable to financial statements. These are described below.

a) **Relevance and Reliability**

Financial statements are expected to provide information that is relevant and will impact the decision making of those who use them. Similarly, they need to provide reliable data. Sometimes it becomes difficult to arrive at an exact estimate, which can hamper the reliability. In such cases, relevance takes precedence, and if the data is expected to provide significant information, it is included with an assumption-based estimate.

b) **Comparability and Consistency**

Financial statements should be comparable across companies in the same industry and sometimes even other industries. This is called comparability. They also need to be consistent in the assumptions and accounting practices over the years so that they can be compared to the previous years' performance. This is called consistency.

c) **Conservatism**

This is a very important concept while recognizing gains and losses. Whenever in doubt, recognize all losses and don't recognize any gains. This gives a pessimistic view to the readers of the financial statements.

d) Materiality

An item that can a cause significant difference in decision making is called a material item. Special care should be taken while including such items. For example, when a company spends $5 for a pen, it does not matter how the company shows it in their financial statement. But if it spends $5 million in buying a land, it should be included as a separate line item.

e) Articulation

The three main parts of the financial statement – Balance Sheet, Income Statement and Statement of Cash Flows are all closely linked. This should be kept in mind while preparing the financial statement. These parts should not be considered separately but treated as an integrated set. This relationship, called Articulation, is shown below.

Figure 4.4

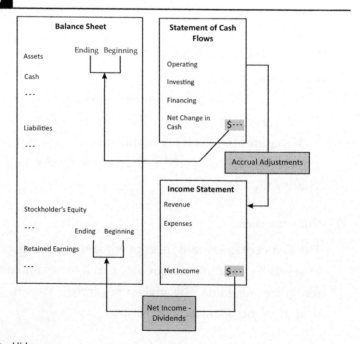

Solved Examples

1. Classify the following items as assets, liabilities or stockholders' equity.

   a. Retained earnings

   b. Cash

   c. Land

   d. Accounts payable

   e. Accounts receivable

Solution:

   a. **Retained earnings** – Stockholders' equity

   b. **Cash** – Asset

   c. **Land** – Asset

   d. **Accounts payable** – Liability

   e. **Accounts receivable** – Asset

2. A company's assets are worth $200,000 and its stockholders' equity equals $150,000. What is the amount of its liabilities?

Solution:

   As per the accounting equation

   Assets = Liabilities + Stockholders' Equity

   Hence, Liabilities = Assets – Stockholders' Equity

   = $200,000 - $150,000

   = $50,000

3. **Classify the below items into Balance Sheet and Income Statement items.**

   a. **Retained earnings**

   b. **Salaries payable**

   c. **Sales**

   d. **Interest earned**

   e. **Land**

Solution:

   a. **Retained earnings** – Balance Sheet as Stockholders' equity

   b. **Salaries payable** – Balance Sheet as Liabilities

   c. **Sales** – Income Statement

   d. **Interest earned** – Income Statement

   e. **Land** – Balance Sheet as Asset

4. **Using the definition of Asset, choose whether the following form an asset.**

   a. **The company has a legal title to a gold mine. The mine has yielded over $1 million of gold. The company's engineers estimate that no further gold is extractable from the mine.**

   b. **The company is currently negotiating the purchase of a building.**

Solution:

    a. Not an asset as it does not provide any economic benefit in the future.

    b. Not an asset as the company does not yet own it and so does not have control over it.

5. **Using the definition of Liability, choose whether the following are liabilities.**

    a. A company contractually guarantees to replace any of its electronic items sold if they don't work as expected within the first year.

    b. The company estimates the total payroll expenses for the coming year to be $500,000.

Solution:

    a. A liability as the company is obligated to replace it in future due to a past transaction.

    b. Not a liability as this is not due to a past transaction. This is different than "Salaries payable". Salaries payable means that the employees have already worked but are yet to be paid. In this case the work has not been done yet – it is only estimated.

Practice Exercise

1. Classify the following items as assets, liabilities or stockholders' equity. If any item does not fall in any of these then state the reason for the same.

   a. Office equipment

   b. Notes payable

   c. Firm's good management

   d. Office supplies

   e. Trademark

   f. Notes receivable

2. A company's liabilities are worth $250,000 and stockholders' equity worth $500,000. Calculate its total assets.

3. ABC Inc. started the month of April with assets worth $1,000,000 and liabilities worth $450,000. During the month of April, stockholders' equity increased by $50,000 and it reduced its liabilities by $40,000. What is the amount of its total assets at the end of April?

4. Classify the following into Balance Sheet and Income Statement items.

   a. Repairs and maintenance

   b. Cost of goods sold

   c. Patents

d. Investment in another company

e. Supplies on hand

f. Salary expense

5. Identify which of the following transactions would be included in the company's Income Statement.

a. Company borrowed $150,000 from the bank

b. A dividend of $5 per share was declared

c. Cash sales worth $5,000 for the month

d. Collection of $10,000 on account from a credit sales made in the previous month

e. Payment of utility bill worth $500

f. Sales made on account worth $10,000

6. Using the definition of Asset, choose which of the following form an asset.

a. The company buys a mining site with an expectation that it has iron ore. It has no other benefit. However, no ore has been found nor is now expected to be present there.

b. The company employs 5 of the world's best engineers recognized in their field.

c. The company claims ownership of a large piece of land. Its current market value is $550 million. The government acquired the land for legal reasons and company employees are not allowed to visit the place.

7. **Using the definition of Liability, choose whether the following form a liability.**

   a. The company got involved in a lawsuit last year. It lost and was ordered to pay $100 million. It has made the payment.

   b. Due to frequent vandalism the company keeps estimates of losses. This year's estimate is that the losses would be worth $1.5 million.

   c. The company obtained services of an accounting firm last year against the obligation of providing them with building security services this year.

Solutions to the above questions can be downloaded from the **Online Resources** *section of this book on* **www.vibrantpublishers.com**

Chapter Summary

◆ A Balance Sheet is a snapshot of a company's source and application of funds on any given date. Companies prepare a balance sheet every quarter and it reflects the company's state on the last day of the quarter.

◆ There are three items that go into a Balance Sheet – Assets, Liabilities & Owners' Equity (also called Stockholders' Equity).

◆ Assets are economic resources of a firm that provide probable future economic benefits due to ownership or control as a result of past transactions or events.

◆ Liabilities are the economic obligations of a firm that require probable future sacrifices of economic benefits, arising from the present obligations of a particular entity to transfer assets or provide services to other entities in the future, as a result of past transactions or events.

◆ Owners' Equity (Stockholders' Equity) is the component that belongs to the owners of the company, which includes shareholders. It contains Paid-in Capital, which refers to the amount directly invested by the owners/stockholders/shareholders. Retained Earnings is another component of equity, which contains the cumulative profits retained by the company over the years. Treasury stock can also appear as part of equity, which includes the amount of money paid by the company for buyback of its own shares. This component will be subtracted from total equity. Balance Sheet is commonly shown using the columnar format.

- *Accounting Equation - Assets = Liabilities + Stockholders' Equity*

- Balance Sheet follows the following concepts and conventions:

  - Entity concept – Every corporation is treated as a separate entity, different from other corporations and also different from its owners or shareholders.

  - Historical costs convention – All assets in the balance are valued at the price at which they were acquired.

  - Going concern – Every balance sheet is prepared on the basis of an assumption that the company will continue to do its business in the future.

- An Income Statement is a statement of the company's revenues and expenses over a period of time – month, quarter, half-year or year. The company's revenue is termed as the "top line" whereas its net income is termed as "bottom line".

- Companies pay out cash dividends to their shareholders. This is a way of sharing profits. However, Dividends do not appear on the Income Statement. They are added after the Income Statement ends (after Net Income).

- Income Statement follows the following concepts and conventions:

  - Time Period Concept – An income statement shows the revenues, expenses and net income over a period of time as against the balance sheet, which shows assets, liabilities and stockholders' equity at a particular point of time.

- Revenue Recognition – Income is recognized when the work is done and money is either collected or is reasonably assured.

- Statement of Cash Flows is the only statement that contains "real" values of money spent or collected. It contains three arts – cash from operating activities, cash from investing activities, and cash from financing activities.

◆ Notes to Financial Statements contain Summary of Significant Accounting Policies, Additional Information about Summary Totals, Disclosure Information Not Recognized, and Supplementary Information.

◆ Apart from the concepts and conventions that are applied separately to the Balance Sheet and Income Statement, there are certain other concepts and conventions that are applicable to financial statements. They are:

- Relevance & Reliability – Financial statements are expected to provide information that is relevant to impact decision making of those who use them. Similarly, they need to provide reliable data.

- Comparability & Consistency – Financial statements should be comparable across companies in the same industry and sometimes, even other industries. They also need to be consistent in the assumptions and accounting practices over years to compare with previous years' performance.

- Conservatism – Whenever in doubt, recognize all losses and don't recognize any gains.

- Materiality – An item that can cause significant difference in decision making is called a material item. Special care should be taken while including such items.

- Articulation – The three main parts of the financial statement – Balance Sheet, Income Statement & Statement of cash flows are all closely linked. This should be kept in mind while preparing them and they should be considered as part of an integrated set.

Chapter 5

The Balance Sheet

In this chapter, our focus is to look at the details inside the balance sheet.

The key learning objectives of this chapter are:

- Understand the terms – assets, liabilities, and equity
- Know the different types of assets – current and long-term
- Know the different types of liabilities – current and long-term
- Know the components of equity
- Learn to make a balance sheet using transaction analysis

The Balance Sheet contains the company's Assets, Liabilities and Stockholders' Equity. The assets and liabilities are further broken down into short-term (current) and long-term assets and liabilities. There can be several items under each of these depending upon the company's line of business. The diagram on the following page shows the most common ones.

Figure 5.1

Balance Sheet

Current assets:
  Cash
  Accounts receivable
  Inventory
  Prepaid Expenses
  Investment Securities
Long-term Assets
  Investments
  Property, plant, and equipment
  Intangible assets
Current Liabilities
  Accounts Payable
  Accrued Liabilities
  Short-term Loans Payable
  Current portion of Long-term Debt
Long-term Liabilities
  Long-term Debt
  Deferred Income Tax Liability
Stockholders' Equity
  Preferred Stock
  Common Stock, par value
  Additional paid-in Capital
  Retained Earnings
  Treasury Stock

5.1 Current Assets

These are the assets that the company intends to use within one year. Below is a description of the various current assets.

Cash

Cash refers to the cash-in-hand or in the company's bank accounts. Companies carry cash to take care of daily operational expenses and also to mitigate risk of low sales, slowdown or recession.

Accounts Receivable

When the company sells products and services to its customers, it may do so without collecting money immediately. The credit period could range from a few days to several months. The amount it expects to receive (within a year) out of the credit extended is shown as a current asset.

Inventory

Companies maintain an inventory of materials, inventory of in-process items (which are still being manufactured) and an inventory of finished goods until they are sold. The value of these inventories is shown as a current asset at cost price (and not at the selling price) as per accounting guidelines discussed earlier under Historical Costs Convention.

Prepaid Expenses

Most companies pay several expenses in advance for the entire year or at least for a few months. The most common examples are rent and insurance premiums. Since these are prepaid, they appear as an asset in the Balance Sheet until the year completes, when they get expensed.

Investment Securities

Companies often park excess cash into short-term investment securities to get higher returns. These are also included in current assets.

5.2 Long-term Assets

Long-term assets are those assets that the company plans to hold onto beyond one year. These are made up of a combination of movable and immovable assets. Immovable assets are almost always of a long-term nature.

Investments

These are similar to investment securities but are of a long-term nature. Companies make long-term investments to earn income or to exercise influence over other companies. Whatever be the purpose, as long as the investment is planned to be kept for more than one year, it appears under long-term assets.

Property, Plant and Equipment (PP&E)

All companies invest in some form of property, plant or equipment. Most of them own an office building or office space. Several manufacturing companies also own plants (manufacturing plants) and equipment (manufacturing equipment). These kinds of assets are almost always of a long-term nature and hence appear under long-term assets. Plants and equipment have a certain life that could range from a few years to several years. Accordingly, they depreciate in value every year. Hence, the company removes the yearly depreciation on these assets before reporting them on the Balance Sheet. This is called Net value of Plant and Equipment. Depreciation cannot be applied to the asset - Land.

Property, plant and equipment:	
Land	$100,000.00
Buildings	$500,000.00
Furniture and fixtures	$80,000.00
Equipment	$150,000.00
Less accumulated depreciation	($25,000.00)
Total property, plant and equipment, net	$805,000.00

Intangible Assets

The assets like trademark, goodwill, patents, etc. are all intangible in nature. But they do provide future benefits and hence should be classified as assets. The challenge is to quantify the value to be included in the Balance Sheet. Hence, the rule is to include only those intangible assets for which the company has actually paid money to acquire. For example, if a company buys another company and pays an amount for goodwill, that amount will be shown as an intangible asset under the head goodwill. Intangible assets lose their value over time and this is shown under Amortization. This concept is similar to depreciation of tangible assets. Hence, the intangible assets, like tangible assets, are shown as net value after subtracting the amortization.

5.3 Current Liabilities

All such liabilities that need to be paid within one year are termed as current liabilities. Below is a description of the most common current liabilities.

Accounts Payable

This is the amount that the company has to pay to its suppliers for credit granted by them. Credit period depends on the industry and company's relative power over its suppliers. In most cases the credit period is within one year and hence this is shown under current liabilities.

Accrued Liabilities

Salary to employees is generally paid at the end of the month or twice a month. Similarly, interest on loans is payable once a month or once a quarter. Even though these have not yet been paid, they will have to be paid in the short-term as they have been accrued. Such accrued expenses are captured under accrued liabilities.

Short-term Loans Payable

Companies wanting money for less than one year may decide to take a short-term loan of a few days up to a year. Since these loans would need to be returned within 1 year they are included under current liabilities.

Current portion of Long-term Debt

Even long-term debt, like mortgages, for example, involve monthly payments. All such payments due within one year are classified under current liabilities.

5.4 Long-term Liabilities

All other liabilities that are not maturing within one year are called long-term liabilities. Below is a description of the most common ones.

Long-term Debt

All companies take long-term loans to finance their long-term investments in property, plant and equipment. These can be in the form of bank loans, long-term bonds, debentures or any other form where a fixed or variable interest is to be paid.

Deferred Income Tax Liability

Due to government taxation rules, several companies are able to prevent payment of taxes immediately. The rules allow them to defer the payment of taxes to a later time. For example, any gain on investment securities is not taxed until the securities are sold even though they have increased in value. Such tax liability is included under long-term liabilities.

5.5 Stockholders' Equity

This is the investment made by the company owners, including stockholders. It also contains the accumulated profits made by the company that belongs to the stockholders. Below are the most common items under this head.

Preferred Stock

Companies can sell preferred stock that gives fixed returns to stockholders. Hence, it is similar to debt. The only difference between preferred stock and debt is that the prior will not lead the company to bankruptcy if the company is unable to pay the fixed dividend. Preferred stock is different than common stock as the preferred stockholders don't have voting rights. Few companies now issue preferred stocks.

Common Stock, par value and Additional paid-in Capital

All common stocks have a par value, which is the face value of the stock. Most companies have it as $1 per stock. Hence, if you pay $20 for a stock, you are actually paying $1 for the par value and $19 for additional paid-up capital. When the company issues common stocks for the first time, it may offer them at $10. It will be reflected as below in the Balance Sheet of the company.

Stockholders' Equity:

Common stock, par value	$1.00
Additional paid-in capital	$19.00

After the initial offering when the stocks are traded on the exchange, this transaction will not have any effect on the company's Balance Sheet. For example, if the $20 stock is sold by the initial stockholder to another person for $30, it will only be a profit for the initial stockholder without any bearing on the company's financial statements.

Retained Earnings

When the company makes a profit, it may pay out some of the profits by way of dividends but retains the rest for investment in assets for further growth. All such profits retained within the company are shown under retained earnings in stockholders' equity. Profits from each year keep adding to the already present retained earnings (a cumulative figure). Similarly, a loss is deducted from the retained earnings and reduces the amount of stockholders' equity.

For example, if the retained earnings are $5,000 and the company has a net income for the year of $500, then the retained earnings become $5,500. Now if the company makes a loss and has a net income of -$100 next year then the retained earnings become $5,400.

Treasury Stock

Profitable companies also distribute profit to shareholders by buying back their stocks at close to market value (most of the times at a premium above the market value). This reduces the company's number of common stocks outstanding and also reduces the amount of stockholders' equity. Treasury stock is always a negative number and is deducted from the total stockholders' equity.

5.6. Transaction Analysis and Balance Sheet Creation

Every financial transaction needs to be reflected in the company's financial statements. But the Balance Sheet contains only a few summarized heads. Hence, putting a transaction under the correct head(s) is important to be able to prepare a Balance Sheet. Below is a template showing some of the common heads under Assets, Liabilities and Stockholders' equity that needs to be used for doing transaction analysis. Additional heads can also be added at appropriate places as needed. It should be noted that for every transaction the accounting equation, Assets = Liabilities + Stockholders' Equity, should hold true. If it does not, then the transaction has been incorrectly recorded.

	Transaction 1	Transaction 2	Transaction 3	Total
Cash	$500.00	($200.00)	$1,000.00	$1,300.00
Inventory				$0.00
Prepaid expenses				$0.00
Property, plant and equipment		$5,000.00		$5,000.00
Total Assets	$500.00	$4,800.00	$1,000.00	$6,300.00
Accounts payable		$4,800.00		$4,800.00
Long-term debt			$1,000.00	$1,000.00
Paid-in Capital	$500.00			$500.00
Total Liabilities and Equity	$500.00	$4,800.00	$1,000.00	$6,300.00

The three transactions described in the above sheet are as follows:

Transaction 1

The company issues stocks worth $500 and receives that money in cash. This increases the cash asset by $500 and also the paid-in capital by $500.

Transaction 2

The company buys property, plant and equipment worth $5,000. It pays only $200 from its cash and agrees to pay the rest on credit later on. This reduces the cash asset by $200 and increases the long-term asset (property, plant and equipment) by $5,000. It also increases the current liability, accounts payable, by $4,800 – the amount of credit the company has taken on this purchase.

Transaction 3

The company decides to take a long-term loan from the bank worth $1,000. This increases its cash asset by $1,000 and increases its long-term debt liability by the same amount.

It may be noted that for each transaction the "Total Assets" column is exactly equal to the "Total Liabilities and Equity" column. It may also be noted that the final value of "Total Assets" is also equal to the final value of "Total Liabilities and Equity". Both of these should always occur for the transactions to have been noted correctly.

The information from the transaction analysis can now be used to create a Balance Sheet as follows.

Balance Sheet January 1, 2021

Current assets:	
Cash	$1,300.00
Long-term assets:	
Property, plant and equipment	$5,000.00
Total assets	$6,300.00
Current liabilities:	
Accounts payable	$4,800.00
Long-term liabilities:	
Long-term debt	$1,000.00
Total liabilities	$5,800.00
Stockholders' equity:	
Paid-in capital	$500.00
Total liabilities and equity	$6,300.00

CASE STUDY:
Case on Balance Sheet – KP Enterprises

Data given below belongs to KP Enterprises.

Transactions from January 1, 2022, the first day of business to January 31, 2022:

a. Initial cash investment by owner: $400,000.

b. Company buys equipment worth $125,000.

c. Borrow cash of $300,000 from the bank @10% per annum, payable every year starting next year. The principal is to be repaid in three years.

d. Purchase of a building and equipment for a total of $750,000. Paid $350,000 in cash and rest will be on mortgage @9% per annum payable yearly from next year onwards. The building is worth $550,000.

e. Inventory purchase of $62,500 with $25,000 in cash and the rest on account.

f. Consulting revenue of $7,500 received in cash for advance of work to be done in the next quarter.

g. Additional amount of $12,500 paid in cash for inventory purchased.

h. Equipment worth $35,000 in lieu of land worth $45,000. Remaining $10,000 will be paid in a month's time.

i. The company did a share buyback worth $40,000.

Case Assignment

i. Analyse all the above transactions using transaction analysis

ii. Make a balance sheet as on 31st January 2022, using the above transaction analysis

Solved Examples

1. Classify the transactions given below into the following categories.

   a. Current assets

   b. Long-term investments

   c. Property, plant and equipment

   d. Intangible assets

   e. Current liabilities

   f. Long-term liabilities

   g. Stockholders' equity

   h. Not a balance sheet item

   Transactions:

   i. Inventory

   ii. Current portion of long-term debt

   iii. Sales

   iv. Stock of another company

   v. Land

   vi. Accounts payable

   vii. Bonds payable

Solution:

   i. **Inventory** – Current assets

   ii. **Current portion of long-term debt** – Current liabilities

   iii. **Sales** – Not a balance sheet item

   iv. **Stock of another company** – Long-term investment

   v. **Land** – Property, plant and equipment

   vi. **Accounts payable** – Current liabilities

   vii. **Bonds payable** – Long-term liabilities

2. **On Jan 1, 2021, the first day of business for ABC Inc., it entered into the following transactions:**

   i. **Initial cash investment by stockholders - $150,000**

   ii. **Purchased equipment for $100,000 in cash.**

   iii. **Traded the equipment for a piece of land worth $60,000. Also received $40,000 cash in the trade.**

   iv. **Borrowed $150,000 cash from the bank at 9% interest rate. Principle and interest are to be paid after four months.**

   v. **Issued $200,000 in bonds in exchange for cash. Interest rate is 10% paid semi-annually. Bonds are for 25 years.**

   vi. **ABC Inc. re-purchased some of the stocks for $40,000**

   vii. **Purchased a building and some equipment for $300,000 in cash. Cost of equipment alone is $190,000.**

Analyze the above transaction and put them in the analysis sheet shown earlier. Prepare a balance sheet for ABC Inc. at the end of Jan 1, 2021.

Solution:

The Analysis sheet will be filled as follows.

	i	ii	iii	iv	v	vi	vii	Total
Cash	$150,000	($100,000)	$40,000	$150,000	$200,000	($40,000)	($300,000)	$100,000
Equipment		$100,000	($100,000)				$190,000	$190,000
Land and Building			$60,000				$110,000	$170,000
Total Assets	$150,000	$0	$0	$150,000	$200,000	($40,000)	$0	$460,000
Bonds					$200,000			$200,000
Bank Loan				$150,000				$150,000
Paid-in Capital	$150,000							$150,000
Treasury stock						($40,000)		
Total Liabilities and Equity	$150,000	$0	$0	$150,000	$200,000	($40,000)	$0	$460,000

a) This is a purely financing transaction of issuing stocks worth $150,000

b) This is buying of equipment for cash.

c) This transaction involves buying an asset in lieu of another asset and some cash.

d) This is a financing transaction. Since this is a new loan, there is no interest liability yet.

e) This is also a financing transaction. Since this is a new bond, there is no interest liability yet.

f) This is a re-purchase of shares that reduces the stockholders' equity.

g) This transaction involves upfront buying of building and equipment with cash.

The Balance Sheet of the company at the end of the day is as follows.

	ABC Inc. Balance Sheet January 1, 2021
Current assets:	
Cash	$100,000
Long-term assets:	
Equipment	$190,000
Land and Building	$170,000
Total assets	$460,000
Current liabilities:	
Bank Loan	$200,000
Long-term liabilities:	
Bonds	$150,000
Total liabilities	$350,000
Stockholders' equity:	
Paid-in capital	$150,000
Treasury stock	($40,000)
Total liabilities and equity	$460,000

3. **The following items are available for the company's fixed assets. Compute the values that will be shown in the balance sheet.**

Land	$100,000
Building	$500,000
Equipment	$250,000
Accumulated depreciation – building	$200,000
Accumulated depreciation – equipment	$100,000

Solution:

A Balance Sheet shows the net value of the assets. In the above case, Land will be shown at its original value, whereas building and equipment will be netted by removing the depreciation and shown as below.

Property, plant and equipment:

Land	$100,000
Building	$500,000
Equipment	$250,000
Less accumulated depreciation	($300,000)
Total property and equipment, net	$550,000

Practice Exercise

1. Classify the transactions given below into the following categories.

   a. Current assets

   b. Long-term investments

   c. Property, plant and equipment

   d. Intangible assets

   e. Current liabilities

   f. Long-term liabilities

   g. Stockholders' equity

   h. Not a balance sheet item

   Transactions

   i.   Rent expense

   ii. Note receivable, due in 5 years

   iii. Additional paid-in capital

   iv. Retained earnings

   v.   Short-term interest earning securities

   vi. Copyright owned by firm

   vii. Cars used for business

   viii. Prepaid insurance

   ix. Accumulated depreciation

   x.   Common stock

2. **Prepare a balance sheet using the following balances.**

Cash in bank accounts	$42,000
Accounts receivable	$55,000
Inventory	$88,000
Investment in 2-month US Treasury securities	$30,000
Long-term investment	$10,000
Land and Building	$300,000
Accumulated depreciation – building	$27,000
Equipment	$64,000
Accumulated depreciation – equipment	$10,000
Patent	$18,000
Long-term note receivable	$16,000
Accounts payable	$66,000
Current portion of long-term debt	$72,000
Long-term debt	$100,000
Common stock, par value	$40,000
Additional paid-in capital	$200,000
Retained earnings	Need to compute

3. **On Jan 1, 2021 its first day of business, XYZ Inc. entered into the following transactions:**

    a. **Initial cash investment by stockholders worth $880,000**

    b. **Purchased equipment for $200,000 in cash.**

    c. **Borrowed $640,000 from the bank at 6% interest rate for 3 years.**

    d. **Bought a building for $2,000,000. Paid $800,000 in cash and the rest on mortgage at 5%. Interest is payable yearly and the term of loan is 10 years.**

    e. **Purchased inventory for $180,000 on account.**

f) **Paid $12,000 for fire insurance of the building for the entire year.**

g) **Paid off $60,000 for the credit on inventory purchased earlier. Analyze the above transaction using the analysis sheet. Prepare a balance sheet at the end of Jan 1, 2021.**

4. **Prepare a balance sheet using the following items.**

Accounts payable	$39,000
Accounts receivable	$51,250
Accumulated depreciation – building	$50,000
Accumulated depreciation – equipment	$6,250
Building	$250,000
Cash	$40,000
Cash for long-term use in restricted account	$12,500
Common stock, par value	$25,000
Equipment	$100,000
Inventory	$50,000
Long-term investment	$12,500
Interest payable	$8,750
Land	$125,000
Long-term note payable	$75,000
Investment securities	$6,250
Retained earnings	$192,500
Short-term loan payable	$26,000
Additional paid-in capital	$225,000

Solutions to the above questions can be downloaded from the **Online Resources** *section of this book on* **www.vibrantpublishers.com**

Chapter Summary

◆ The Balance Sheet contains the company's Assets, Liabilities and Stockholders' Equity. The assets and liabilities are further broken up into short-term (called current) and long-term assets and liabilities.

◆ Current Assets are those assets that the company intends to use within 1 year. Commonly seen current assets are cash, accounts receivable, inventory, prepaid expenses, and investment securities.

◆ Long-term Assets are those assets that the company will use over a period longer than 1 year. Commonly seen long-term assets are investments, property, plant, and equipment, and intangible assets.

◆ Liabilities that need to be paid within 1 year are termed as current liabilities. Commonly seen current liabilities are accounts payable, accrued liabilities, short-term loans payable, and current portion of long-term debt.

◆ All other liabilities that do not mature within 1 year are called long-term liabilities. Commonly seen long-term liabilities are long-term debt and deferred income tax liability.

◆ Stockholder's Equity is the investment made by the company owners, including stockholders. It also contains the accumulated profits made by the company that belongs to the stockholders. It may consist of the headings – preferred stock, common stock, paid-in capital, retained earnings, and treasury stock.

◆ *Accounting Equation - Assets = Liabilities + Stockholders' Equity*

◆ We can make a Balance Sheet by using Transaction Analysis based on the accounting equation.

Chapter **6**

The Income Statement

I n this chapter, we take a detailed look at the income statement.

The key learning objectives of this chapter are:

- Understand the various parts of an income statement
- Know the different types of revenues
- Know the different types of expenses
- Understand the concept and timing of revenue and expense recognition
- Learn to make an income statement using transaction analysis

Income statement contains the revenue and expenses transactions over a period of time – generally a quarter or a year. A balance sheet is a snapshot, whereas, an income statement is a running log. Like different types of assets and liabilities on the balance sheet, there are different kinds of revenues and expenses on the income statement. There are also several interim values in the income statement that carry importance. The diagram below shows all the major terms in an income statement.

Figure 6.1

Income Statement

Sales

- Cost of Goods Sold

= Gross Profit

- Other Operating Expenses, Gains and Losses

= Operating Income (EBIT)

- Interest Expense

= Income before Taxes (PBT)

- Income Tax Expense

= Income from Continuing Operations

+/- Income from Discontinued Operations

+/- Extraordinary Items

+/- Cumulative Effect of Accounting Changes

= Net Income (PAT

6.1 Measures of Income

As seen above, there are various ways we can use to measure a company's income. Each of them conveys different information about a company's revenue and expenses. Below is a description of these measures.

Gross Profit

For a company selling products, gross profit is the difference between the selling price and the cost price of the product. For example, for a car manufacturer, gross profit is the difference between the price of the car at which the company sells to the dealer and the cost of manufacturing it. Similarly, for a grocery store, it is the difference between the price at which the store sells groceries and the wholesale cost at which it buys it.

Operating Income (EBIT)

Every company has overheads related to administrative, selling, marketing, and other functions. When all these are removed from the gross profit, we get another important measure of profit called Operating Income or Earnings before Interest and Tax (EBIT).

Income (Profit) before Taxes (PBT)

Companies that have any kind of debt financing have an interest expense to pay. They can be bank loans, bonds, preferred stock, or any other such financing that pays interest. The only financing that does not have interest payments is common equity. When the interest expense is subtracted from EBIT, we get Income before Taxes or Profit before Taxes (PBT).

Income from Continuing Operations

After removing the income tax expense we get the bottom line called as Income from Continuing Operations. The items that this profit measure does not include are called "below the line items" – Income from discontinued operations, extraordinary items and cumulative effect of accounting changes.

Below the Line Items

Income from Discontinued Operations is reported when the revenue is generated by a part of business that is being discontinued. For example, when a retail chain plans to close a store in the year, it will report revenue from that store under this head.

Extraordinary Items are those items that are of a one-time nature and the company does not expect to encounter them on a regular basis in the future. For example, a big loss due to a natural disaster like a fire or an earthquake would be shown under this head.

Cumulative Effect of Accounting Changes refers to any changes in the income due to change in the assumptions made while making the financial statements and, hence, are not considered to be a regular business income or expense.

Net Income (PAT)

In most cases the Net Income or Profit after Tax (PAT) will be same as Income from Continuing Operations as the "below the line items" are not always present. This is the final measure of profit and this is what is seen by most companies, investors and analysts while analyzing a company's profitability.

6.2 Types of Revenues

Although we have shown revenue as a single item in the above example Income Statement, it can be from several sources. Accordingly, we may show them separately as several items. Below are the most common sources of revenue.

Sales Revenue

This revenue is generated when a company sells its products. For example, an automobile company generates sales revenue when it sells its cars.

Service Revenue

Companies in the services business generate revenue under this head by selling services. For example, an accounting firm generates this revenue through its consulting business.

Interest Revenue

This revenue can be a small component for some companies who have simply parked extra cash to generate some interest income. However, this could be a major source of revenue for banks.

6.3 Types of Expenses

As there are several streams of revenue, there are also several streams of expenses. Below is a description of the most common expenses.

Cost of Goods Sold

This is the cost of manufacturing of the product sold by the company. For a car manufacturer, this is how much it costs to build a car, and for a retailer, it is the wholesale cost of apparel.

Selling, General, and Administrative Expenses

These are all the expenses incurred for administrative, sales and marketing work in the company, which cannot be directly tied to any particular sale. These are mostly the indirect expenses of the company.

Research and Development (R&D) Expense

Although R&D brings about future benefits, it is not reported as an asset. This is because it is difficult to estimate the value it can bring in future and hence leaves a lot to individual judgment. Hence, this expense is reported in the income statement under R&D expense head.

Wages and Salary Expense

This includes all payroll related expenses, including all employee benefits, pensions, healthcare etc.

Bad Debt Expense

When some debtors do not pay the company, partly or fully, that amount is reported under this head in the income statement.

Depreciation

Buildings and equipment are allowed to depreciate over a period of time based on their expected life as discussed in the previous chapter. This means that they are depreciated every year until they are totally consumed. Each year, the depreciation is calculated and reported in the Income Statement and also subtracted from the gross value of Property, Plant and Equipment in the balance sheet to give a net value of Property, Plant and Equipment. Depreciation is done using one of two methods – straight-line depreciation method and double-declining balance method. In straight-line depreciation, the depreciation amount used every year will be equal for the entire life of the asset. In double-declining balance method it is higher in the early years and reduces later on. Below is an example of an asset with a cost of $40,000 with life of five years.

Cost = $40,000

Residual value = $4,000 (estimated resale value expected after 5 years)

Useful life = 5 years

Straight Line depreciation = (Cost – Residual value)/Useful life = ($40,000 - $4,000)/5 = $7,200

Double-declining balance depreciation = Book Value * Fixed percentage every year

For year 1 with 40%, it will be = $40,000 * 0.4 = $16,000

For year 2 with 40%, it will be = ($40,000 - $16,000) * 0.4 = $9,600

The depreciation under the two types would look like this:

Year			Accumulated Depreciation		Book Value	
	Straight Line	Double declining-balance	Straight Line	Double declining-balance	Straight Line	Double declining-balance
1	$7,200	$16,000	$7,200	$16,000	32,800	$24,000
2	$7,200	$9,600	$14,400	$25,600	$25,600	$14,400
3	$7,200	$5,760	$21,600	$31,360	$18,400	$8,640
4	$7,200	$3,456	$28,800	$34,816	$11,200	$5,184
5	$7,200	$1,184	$36,000	$36,000	$4,000	$4,000

In the last year, the depreciation under double-declining balance would be equal to whatever is remaining over and above the residual value of $4,000.

Interest Expense

This is the amount of money the company pays for its debt and preferred stock.

Income Tax Expense

This is the amount of money the company needs to pay to government by way of income tax.

6.4 Earnings per Share (EPS) and Diluted EPS

This is a very important measure shown on the Income Statement after the Net Income. It is calculated by dividing Net Income by Total Number of Common Stock of the company. It gives an idea of how much value per share the company has added in the year.

There is also another measure called, Diluted Earnings per Share (Diluted EPS) which is mentioned below EPS. If the company has pledged stock options to its employees or others, then it takes those into account while calculating Diluted EPS.

For example, if the company's Net Income is $500 and it has 500 shares outstanding, then its EPS = $1. But if the company also has pledged stock options of 100 shares to its employees, then its Diluted EPS = 0.833 ($500/600).

6.5 Revenue Recognition

Suppose you have sold a product to a customer, who will pay for it after three months. Should you recognize revenue now or three months later? Similarly, suppose you receive an advance payment for work that is to be done after one month. Should the revenue be recognized now or after one month?

In order to answer the above questions, there are two criteria that help determine when to recognize revenue. They are as follows:

a) The promised work must be done before revenue is recognized

b) Cash collection should be reasonably assured before revenue is recognized

As per the above criteria, revenue should not be recognized before the work is completed but can be recognized before money is collected, as long as it is assured. Below are some examples of revenue recognition.

a) A grocery store sells items for immediate cash payment. Hence, revenue is recognized as soon as a sale is made.

b) Some retailers provide a credit period when customers buy home appliances. In this case, even though the goods are delivered, the payment is not made immediately. Here, retailer has two options. The first option is to recognize the revenue immediately if the payment is assured and the second option is to or recognize it in parts as the payment is made.

c) An airlines company asks customers to pay for their ticket in advance at the time of booking even though the flight is actually after a few months. In this case, the airline does not recognize revenue until it has actually completed the work of transporting the customer.

d) Football season tickets are paid for in advance, but revenue is recognized gradually as the season progresses.

e) Software product vendors sell their software along with 1-year warranty support. Here, some part of the revenue is recognized at the time of sales and the rest over a period of time as the support nears its end.

6.6 Expense Recognition

As we saw above, revenue is recognized based on the two criteria explained above. The expense incurred to provide that product or service also needs to follow some rules to ensure that it gets recognized along with the revenue. If this does not happen, then the net income calculation might be incorrect. In most cases the "matching concept" is used to recognize expense. This means that the expense is matched with revenue and recognized together. This makes sense for direct expenses but cannot be used with overheads like sales and promotion expenses. These expenses are recognized immediately as they cannot be matched directly with any revenue. Yet another way of recognizing revenue is depreciation. Capital equipment and buildings depreciate over a period of time and this depreciation is carried over in pre-determined instalments every year in the Income Statement. This is again because their expense cannot be directly matched with revenue and also cannot be immediately expensed when they become assets of the company. To summarize, below are the three ways of expense recognition:

a) Direct matching, as with cost of goods sold

b) Immediate recognition, as with advertising

c) Systematic allocation, as with depreciation

6.7 Expanded Accounting Equation

As seen above, the accounting equation is as follows:

Assets = Liabilities + Equity

However, Equity = Paid-in capital + Retained earnings

Now, Retained Earnings gets computed on the basis of how much profit or loss the company makes. In the previous chapter we have seen that, Retained Earnings = Net Income – Dividends.

This can be further broken up into,

Retained Earnings = (Revenues – Expenses) – Dividends

So, we finally have,

Equity = Paid-in Capital + (Revenues – Expenses) – Dividends

This is the expanded form of the accounting equation.

The next section shows transaction analysis using this expanded equation.

6.8 Transaction Analysis and Income Statement Creation

The following transaction sheet template can be used for analyzing financial transactions and it finally helps prepare an Income Statement. It is similar to the one used earlier for preparing a Balance Sheet with three additions – Revenue, Expenses and Dividends. Please note that some of the heads under assets have been omitted to make the sheet fit on the page. Similarly, all the revenue streams – sales revenue, services revenue and interest revenue are clubbed together into a single head called Revenue to save space. All expenses are also clubbed together under a general Expense head. In reality they can be Cost of Goods Sold, Interest expense, Wages, Depreciation etc.

	Transaction 1	Transaction 2	Transaction 3	Total
Cash	$1,000.00	($200.00)	($250.00)	$550.00
Inventory	($700.00)			($700.00)
Total Assets	$300.00	($200.00)	($250.00)	($150.00)
Accounts payable				$0.00
Long-term debt				$0.00
Paid in capital				$0.00
Revenue	$1,000.00			$1,000.00
Expense	($500.00)	($200.00)		($700.00)
Dividends			($250.00)	($250.00)
Total Liabilities and Equity	$500.00	($200.00)	($250.00)	$50.00

The three transactions described in the above sheet are as follows:

Transaction 1

Company sells goods worth $500 for $1,000. This results in $1,000 revenue. Applying the matching concept, the expense of $500 is immediately applied. This expense is actually Cost of Goods Sold. Due to this transaction, the company also receives $1,000 in cash and its inventory reduces by $500. It is important to note here that the reduction in inventory should match the Cost of Goods Sold expense as inventory is shown at cost price.

Transaction 2

This is a transaction where the company pays out interest on its loans. The $200 expense is actually Interest expense. It also reduces the cash by an equal amount.

Transaction 3

In this transaction the company pays out $250 dividend to its shareholders. This also reduces the cash by an equal amount.

It may again be noted that in each of the above transactions the expanded accounting equation holds true. The income statement based on the above transactions is as below.

Revenues		
Sales		$1,000.00
Expenses:		
Cost of goods sold	$500.00	
Interest expense	$200.00	
Total expenses		$700.00
Net Income		$300.00
Dividends		$250.00

It should be noted that although Dividends are shown in the above income statement, they are actually not a part of the income statement. The income statement ends at Net Income. Dividends are mentioned after that to provide enough information about retained earnings.

CASE STUDY:
Case on Income Statement – Trader's Home Inc

The various account heads of Trader's Home Inc. for the year ended December 31, 2021 are given below.

Promotion expenses	$2,500
Retained earnings (beginning balance)	$50,000
COGS	$40,000
Transportation expenses	$6,000
Depreciation	$5,000
Insurance expenses	$1,000
Interest expenses	$200
Miscellaneous expenses	$2,500
Revenue	$90,000
Salary and wages	$4,000
Dividends	$1,000
Consumables expenses	$750
Income tax rate	25%

Case Assignment

i. Prepare an income statement for the year 2021 based on the values given above.

ii. If the company's paid-in capital is $75,000, what will be its stockholder's equity on 31st December 2021?

Solved Examples

1. Classify the given items under the following heads found in the Income Statement.

   a. Revenue

   b. Cost of goods sold

   c. Selling, general, and administrative expense

   d. Other income statement item

   e. Not an income statement item

   The items to classify are as below.

   i. Prepaid insurance

   ii. Restructuring charge

   iii. Interest payable

   iv. Sales

   v. Gain on sale of land

   vi. Taxes payable

   vii. Advertising expense

Solution:

   i. **Prepaid insurance** – Not an income statement item. This is an asset in the balance sheet.

   ii. **Restructuring charge** – Other income statement item.

   iii. **Interest payable** – Not an income statement item. This is a liability in the balance sheet.

iv. **Sales** – Revenue.

v. **Gain on sale of land** – Other income statement item. Comes under Gains and Losses.

vi. **Taxes payable** – Not an income statement item. This is a liability in the balance sheet.

vii.**Advertising expense** – Selling, general, and administrative expense.

2. **Indicate whether the following items fall under Revenue, Expense, Gain or Loss.**

   a. **Interest earned on short-term investment**

   b. **Retail price of goods sold**

   c. **Fees received in exchange for providing a service**

   d. **Wholesale cost of goods sold**

Solution:

   a. **Interest earned on short-term investment** – Revenue

   b. **Retail price of goods sold** – Revenue. This is the selling price.

   c. **Fees received in exchange for providing a service** – Revenue

   d. **Wholesale cost of goods sold** – Expense. This is the cost of goods sold.

3. **XYZ Inc. has the following transactions in 2021. Prepare an Income Statement for the firm.**

   a. **Insurance expense $15,000**

   b. **Advertising expense $60,000**

   c. **Salary and wages $100,000**

   d. **Equipment rental revenue $600,000**

   e. **Interest earned on idle cash $2,000**

   f. **Other expenses $45,000**

   g. **Rental revenue for idle warehouse $40,000**

   h. **Income tax expense @25% of income before taxes**

   The company also has 1,000,000 common shares outstanding. Calculate the EPS.

Solution:

The Income Statement should have all the revenues on top followed by all the expenses. However, we would first need to compute the Profit before Tax (PBT) and then calculate the Income Tax expense. We would finally get the Net Income or Profit after Tax (PAT).

XYZ Inc.

Income Statement for 2021

Revenues:

Equipment rental revenue	$600,000.00
Warehouse rental revenue	$40,000.00
Interest revenue	$40,000.00
Total revenues	$642,000.00

Expenses:

Salary and Wages	$100,000.00
Insurance expense	$15,000.00
Advertising expense	$ 60,000.00
Other expenses	$45,000.00
Total expenses	$220,000.00
Profit before Tax	$422,000.00
Income Tax @25%	$105,500.00
Net Income	$316,500.00
Common shares outstanding	1,000,000.00
EPS	$0.3165

5. **XYZ Inc. has begun the year with the following account balances:**

Cash	$5,000
Accounts receivable	$14,000
COGS	$40,000
Inventory	$11,000
Accounts payable	$8,000
Paid-in capital	$7,000
Retained earnings	$15,000

During the year the following transactions took place. Use the transaction analysis worksheet and prepare the Income Statement and Balance Sheet for the company.

i. **Sales of $225,000, 90% on account**

ii. **Cash collections on receivable of $200,000**

iii. **Purchased inventory on account for $180,000**

iv. **Cost of inventory sold $175,000**

v. **Paid accounts payable $173,000**

vi. **Paid misc expenses $37,000**

Solution:

The given analysis sheet shows the above transactions.

	Opening Balance	i	ii	iii	iv	v	vi	Total
Cash	$5,000	$22,500	$200,000			($173,000)	($37,000)	$17,500
Accounts receivable	$14,000	$202,500	($200,000)					$16,500
Inventory	$11,000			$180,000	($175,000)			$16,000
Total Assets	$30,000	$225,000	$0	$180,000	($175,000)	($173,000)	($37,000)	$50,000
Accounts payable	$8,000			$180,000		($173,000)		$15,000
Paid-in Capital	$7,000							$7,000
Retained earnings	$15,000							$15,000
Sales		$225,000						$225,000
Cost of goods sold					($175,000)			($175,000)
Misc. expense							($37,000)	($37,000)
Total Liabilities and Equity	$30,000	$225,000	$0	$180,000	($175,000)	($173,000)	($37,000)	$50,000

The company's Income Statement is as below.

XYZ Inc.

Income Statement for 2021

Revenues:	
Sales	$225,000.00
Total revenues	$225,000.00
Expenses:	
Cost of goods sold	$175,000.00
Misc. expenses	$ 37,000.00
Total expenses	$212,000.00
Net Income	$13,000.00

The company's Balance Sheet is as below.

XYZ Inc.

Balance Sheet January 1, 2021

Current assets:	
Cash	$17,500
Accounts receivable	$16,500
Inventory	$16,000
Total assets	$50,000
Current liabilities:	
Accounts payable	$15,000
Total liabilities	$15,000
Stockholders' equity:	
Paid-in capital	$7,000
Retained earnings*	**$28,000**
Total liabilities and equity	$50,000

Retained earnings is a cumulative figure. Last year it was $15,000. This year the Net Income will be added to it to make it $28,000.

Below is the formula.

Retained earnings (2021) = Retained earnings (2020) + Net Income (2021) – Dividends (2021)

Practice Exercise

1. Classify the given items under the following heads found in the Income Statement.

   a. Revenue

   b. Cost of goods sold

   c. Selling, general, and administrative expense

   d. Other income statement item

   e. Not an income statement item

   The items (to classify) are as below.

   i. Delivery expense

   ii. Income tax expense

   iii. CEO's salary

   iv. Dividends paid

   v. Sales commission paid

   vi. Supplies on hand

   vii. Gain on sale of land

   viii. Depreciation expense

2. Indicate whether the following items fall under Revenue, Expense, Gain or Loss.

   a. Sale of delivery truck for more than its purchase price

   b. Sale of land for less than its purchase price

   c. Estimated amount of accounts receivable created this year that will be uncollectible

   d. Destruction of warehouse in fire

3. XYZ Inc. has the following transactions in 2021. Prepare an Income Statement for the firm.

   a. Sales worth $200,000

   b. All items were priced at 1.25 times their cost

   c. Salary and wages were 5% of sales

   d. Insurance expense $2,000

   e. Other expenses were 1% of cost of goods sold

   f. Advertising and promotion expense were 2% of sales

   g. Income tax expense @30% of income before taxes

The company also has 500,000 common shares outstanding. Calculate the EPS.

3. XYZ Inc. has the following transactions in 2021. Prepare an Income Statement for the firm.

   a. Sales worth $200,000

   b. All items were priced at 1.25 times their cost

   c. Salary and wages were 5% of sales

   d. Insurance expense $2,000

   e. Other expenses were 1% of cost of goods sold

   f. Advertising and promotion expense were 2% of sales

   g. Income tax expense @30% of income before taxes

The company also has 500,000 common shares outstanding. Calculate the EPS.

4. ZZZ company began the year with the following balances:

Cash	$15,000
Accounts receivable	$42,000
Inventory	$33,000
Accounts payable	$24,000
Paid-in capital	$45,000
Retained earnings	$21,000

The following transaction took place during the year. Analyze them using the transaction analysis sheet and prepare the company's Income Statement and Balance Sheet.

a. Borrowed $30,000 on a long term loan.

b. Interest expense for the year $3,000. This amount has not yet been paid.

c. Sales for the year was $500,000, all on account.

d. Cash collections on account receivable $280,000

e. Purchased inventory on account $380,000

f. Cost of inventory sold was $350,000

g. Paid accounts payable $173,000

h. Paid wage expense $137,000

Chapter Summary

◆ Income Statement consists of Revenue, Gross Profit, Operating Income (EBIT – Earnings Before Interest and Tax), Profit Before Tax (PBT), and Net Income (PAT – Profit After Tax).

◆ Gross Profit is the difference between the selling price and cost price of a product. When we remove all the other expenses, except interest and tax, we get EBIT. Further subtraction of interest expense gives PBT and if we also subtract tax, then we get PAT.

◆ Revenue can be from products (called Sales Revenue) or services (called Service Revenue). Any revenue earned through interest received due to investments is termed as Interest Revenue.

◆ COGS (Cost of Goods Sold) is an expense that includes only the cost price of the product. SGA (Selling, General, and Administrative Expenses) includes all other sales related expenses.

◆ R&D (Research & Development) expenses are all the expenses incurred for research related work. Wages and Salary expense is related to the company's payroll. Bad Debt is a head used to include expenses for money that was not received from a sale. Depreciation expense includes depreciation of long-term physical assets. Interest expense and Income Tax expense include the money spent to pay interest on loans and money paid as income tax respectively.

◆ Earnings per share (EPS) is a calculated as Net Income divided by the Total Number of Shares. Diluted EPS could be different than EPS, if the company has pledged stock options to its employees.

◆ Revenue is recognized when the work is completed and the money is reasonably assured. Expense is recognized either in the same period as the associated revenue, or immediately, when there is no associated revenue, or systematically for expenses like depreciation.

◆ Expanded Accounting Equation - *Assets = Liabilities + Paid-in capital + (Revenues – Expenses) – Dividends*

◆ We can make an Income Statement by using Transaction Analysis based on the expanded accounting equation.

This page is intentionally left blank

Chapter 7

The Statement of Cash Flows

In this chapter, we shall look at the statement of cash flows.

The key learning objectives of this chapter are:

- Understand the various parts of a statement of cash flows

- Know the different cash flow patterns of different types of companies

- Understand the methods for preparing the statement of cash flows

Values that go in the Balance Sheet and Income statement are estimates based on some underlying assumptions. Hence, they may not give the right picture. As against this, the statement of cash flows is completely realistic. It shows how much cash comes in and goes out of the company's bank accounts. It does not have any assumptions. Hence, it gives a more realistic picture of how a company is doing.

7.1 Categories of Cash Flow Activities

Both Balance Sheet and Income Statement contain one single figure, like Total Assets, Total Liabilities and Equity, or Net Income that is generally looked at. However, Cash Flow statement contains three independent items that are looked at. They fall under the following categories:

a)   Operating activities

b)   Investing activities

c)   Financing activities

All financial transactions that involve a cash flow (not on credit) are classified under of these categories. They are accordingly placed in separate parts of the statement of cash flows and have separate significance. The sections below describe each of these categories.

Operating Activities

Any cash inflow or outflow from the company's regular business activities is called Operating Cash Flow. This includes cash collected from customers from the sale of goods or services and cash paid to suppliers and employees for their goods and services. Cash inflows from interest and dividend income due to the company's investments also fall under this category. Operating activities are all those activities that are related to current assets and liabilities, except those liabilities which are related to financing, like loans.

The following activities fall under Operating activities.

Figure 7.1

Cash inflow:
Sale of goods or services
Sale of trading securities
Interest revenue
Dividend revenue

Cash outflow:
Inventory purchases
Wages and salaries
Taxes
Interest expense
Other expenses (utility bills, rent etc.)
Purchase of trading securities

Investing Activities

Companies invest in long-term assets like property, plant, and equipment, long-term investment in other companies and giving out loans to other companies. All activities related to these investing activities come under Investing Cash Flow. Below are the activities under Investing activities.

Figure 7.2

Cash inflow:
Sale of plant
Sale of land or building
Sale of equipment
Sale of business segment
Sale of non-trading securities
Collection of principal on loans

Cash outflow:
Purchase of plant
Purchase of land or building
Purchase of equipment
Purchase of non-trading securities
Extending loans to other entities

Financing Activities

Companies finance using various means, like common stock, preferred stock, and debt. They may also pay cash dividends to shareholders. All of these financing activities are seen under Financing Cash Flow. It is worth noting that cash dividends paid by the company are part of financing activities whereas, interest expense is a part of operating activities. Below are all the financing activities.

Figure 7.3

Cash inflow:
Issuance of common stock
Issuance of preferred stock
Debt (loans, bonds, notes mortgages etc.)

Cash outflow:
Cash dividends
Repayment of debt
Repurchase of stock (treasury stock)

7.2 Cash Flow Pattern

The normal pattern of net cash flow for a company is as below:

a) Net cash inflow from Operating activities +

b) Net cash outflow in Investing activities -

c) Net cash inflow/outflow from Financing activities +/-

Positive cash flow from operations is important for all companies, except for start-ups. Cash outflow into investing activities is generally seen in companies as they create assets for future growth. Depending upon whether a company is able to finance all its investments using its operating cash flow or not, its cash flow from financing activities will be either positive or negative.

Below is a typical cash flow for companies at various stages.

Start-up Company

Since these companies don't have much business, most of their cash flow needs are from financing activities, which feed into both operating and investment needs.

Figure 7.4

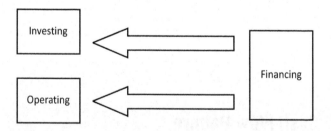

Steady-state Company

A well settled company generates enough cash from operations to use the cash in investing and also to pay dividends for common and preferred stocks.

Figure 7.5

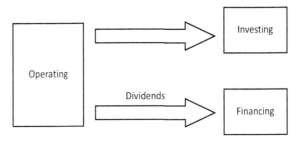

Cash Cow

A cash cow is a company that generates enough cash to use in investing and for repayment of loans, share repurchases and payment of dividends.

Figure 7.6

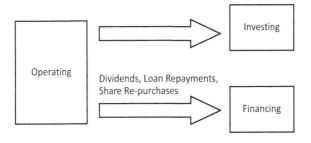

7.3 Cash Flow Statement Preparation

The statement of cash flows can be prepared using two different methods:

a)   Direct method and

b)   Indirect method.

Direct method uses transaction analysis in the same way as was done for preparing balance sheet and income statement. However, it is a less common method. Most companies create the cash flow statement using the indirect method. Below are the two methods.

Direct Method

All the transactions are analyzed and the ones involving cash inflow or outflow are captured and put in the statement of cash flows as below.

Transactions:

1.   Sales on account for $10,000

2.   Collections on account for $12,000

3.   Purchased inventory on account for $8,000

4.   Cost of goods sold is $8,000

5.   Paid accounts payable worth $7,500

6.   Purchased property, plant, and equipment worth $4,000

7.   Sold property, plant, and equipment for $1,500 cash

8.   Repaid a bank loan worth $500

9. Issued new stock worth $1,000 and collected cash

10. Depreciation expense of $400

11. Interest payment of $250 in cash

12. Interest accrued is worth $50

13. Wages and supplies expenses worth $1,500 paid in cash

14. Recorded income tax expense of $500

15. Paid income tax of $400

The following table splits the above transactions into cash and non-cash transactions. It also classifies the cash transactions into operating, investing and financing. This will help to further compute the three categories of cash flows.

Table 7.1

Tran #	Cash/ Non-cash	Type	Cash flow	Comments
1	Non-cash	-	-	This is a credit sale
2	Cash	Operating	$12,000	Cash is collected against accounts receivable
3	Non-cash	-	-	This is a credit buy
4	Non-cash	-	-	No cash is paid for the goods. The expense is only recognized now.
5	Cash	Operating	-$7,500	Cash is paid against accounts payable
6	Cash	Investing	-$4,000	This is a cash buy of PP&E
7	Cash	Investing	$1,500	This is a cash sale of PP&E
8	Cash	Financing	-$500	This is cash payment for loan
9	Cash	Financing	$1,000	This is a cash receipt from new stock
10	Non-cash	-	-	Depreciation is not a cash expense
11	Cash	Operating	-$250	This is a cash outflow for interest on loan
12	Non-cash	-	-	Accrual is not a cash expense
13	Cash	Operating	-$1,500	This is cash paid for work
14	Non-cash	-	-	Only recording is not a cash expense
15	Cash	Operating	-$400	This is cash paid for tax

Once the above has been captured, the Statement of Cash Flows can be prepared as below. It may be noted that operating, investing and financing activities are recorded separately on the statement of cash flows.

Statement of Cash Flows

For Year ended December 31, 2020

Cash flows from Operating Activities:	
Cash	$12,000
Payment for inventory purchase	($7,500)
Payment for misc. expenses	($1,500)
Payment of interest	($250)
Payment of income tax	($400)
Net cash provided by Operating Activities	$2,350
Cash flows from Investing Activities:	
Purchase of PP&E	($4,000)
Sale of PP&E	$1,500
Net cash used by Investing Activities	($2,500)
Cash flows from Financing Activities:	
Stock issue	$1,000
Repayment of long-term debt	($500)
Net cash provided by Financing Activities	$500
Net increase in cash*	**$350**
Beginning cash balance*	**$250**
Ending cash balance*	**$600**

*In the above statement of cash flows, the last three lines summarize the cash positions. The "Net Increase in cash" is computed by adding the net cash values of operating, investing and financing activities. The "Beginning cash balance" is directly picked up from the Balance Sheet of last year. The "Ending cash balance" is computed by adding net increase in cash to beginning cash balance.

Indirect Method

This method starts from the other financial statements, namely Balance Sheet and Income Statement. Using the data in these two, the Statement of Cash Flows is prepared. In order to do so we would need the Balance Sheet for the previous year as well to view changes in the various items.

This method is a little more complex but due to the use of computers, it is preferred by most companies as it does not need any additional information to create other than the availability of balance sheet and income statement. Readers of statement of cash flows prepared using this method might find it a little more difficult to read but the advantage of this method is that it gives insights into where the money is going.

Step 1 – Get Balance Sheet (two years), Income Statement (one year) and Notes to Financial Statements

The first requirement to prepare statement of cash flows using this method is the availability of balance sheet and income statement. Given below are example balance sheet (for two years) and income statement (for one year only).

Balance Sheet	2020	2019
Current assets:		
Cash	$1,630	$500
Accounts receivable	$1,800	$2,300
Inventory	$1,900	$2,000
Long-term assets:		
Property, plant, and equipment	$4,500	$4,000
Less accumulated depreciation	$1,000	$1,300
Property, plant, and equipment - net	$3,500	$2,700
Total assets	$8,830	$7,500
Current liabilities:		
Accounts payable	$2,000	$2,200
Taxes payable	$100	$80
Interest payable	$20	$0
Long-term liabilities:		
Long-term debt	$2,500	$3,000
Stockholders' equity:		
Common stock	$1,000	$500
Retained earnings	$3,210	$1,720
Total liabilities and equity	$8,830	$7,500

Income Statement For 2020	
Sales	$15,000
Gain on sale of equipment	$100
Expenses:	
Cost of goods sold	$10,000
Misc. expenses	$2,760
Depreciation expense	$460
Interest expense	$100
Total Expenses	$13,320
Income before taxes	$1,780
Income tax expense	$290
Net Income	$1,490

The Notes to the Financial Statement of 2020 mentions the following activities of buying and selling property, plant, and equipment.

Sold PP&E worth $540 and bought PP&E worth $1,700

Step 2 – Identification of increase and decrease in all current assets and liabilities

The following table shows increases and decreases in the current assets and liabilities from 2019 to 2020 by using the values from the balance sheet.

Table 7.2

Item	Type	Nature of change	Change
Cash	Current Asset	Increase	$1,130
Accounts receivable	Current Asset	Decrease	$500
Inventory	Current Asset	Decrease	$100
Accounts payable	Current Liability	Decrease	$200
Tax payable	Current Liability	Increase	$20
Interest payable	Current Liability	Increase	$20

Step 3 – Identify non-cash expenses, gains and losses

Under the indirect method operating cash flow starts with the Net Income for the year. We then add non-cash expenses to it as no cash has actually been spent on such expenses. In most cases it is only the depreciation expense. In some cases, amortization is also to be considered if present in the balance sheet and expense statement. In this case, only depreciation is present.

Gains and losses on long-term assets like property, plant and equipment are also to be adjusted in the operating cash flows. Any gain is subtracted and loss is added. Hence, if a gain is made in selling a long-term asset, then the gain amount is to be deducted from the cash flows from operating activities. This is simply because such a gain will be considered later on in the cash flows from investing activities. If we don't adjust the amount here then it would lead to double counting in operating as well as investing cash flows. We have a gain on PP&E mentioned in the income statement.

Step 4 – Preparing cash flow from operating activities

The idea of preparing this cash flow is to make adjustments to cash on the basis of how much cash has been consumed or recovered from current assets and liabilities. For example, if inventory increases, additional amount of cash gets blocked and, hence, that additional amount needs to be subtracted from the Net Income. Similarly, if the accounts payable increases, it means that the company has managed to get additional credit which has saved cash. Hence, this difference will be added to the Net Income. In this way all the increases and decreases in current assets and liabilities identified in the previous step are either subtracted or added to the Net Income to get the cash flow from operating activities as below.

Cash flows from Operating activities:

Net Income		$1,490
Add depreciation expense	$460	
Gain on sale of PP&E	($100)	
Decrease in accounts receivable	$500	
Decrease in inventory	$100	
Decrease in accounts payable	($200)	
Increase in tax payable	$20	
Increase in interest payable	$20	
		$800
Net cash provided by Operating activities		$2,290

It may be noted that the above statement does not take into account the increase in Cash as a current asset. When the entire statement of cash flows is completed it will show this change. Cash is the only current asset that does not appear in the cash flows from operating activities. It is the outcome of the entire cash flow statement and hence it appears at the end.

Step 5 – Preparing cash flow from investing activities

There is no change in any long-term assets other than PP&E. The Notes above mention these changes. Hence, it is straight forward to create cash flows from investing activities as below.

Cash flows from Investing activities:

Sold PP&E	$540
Purchased PP&E	($1,700)
Cash flows from Investing activities:	($1,160)

Step 6 – Preparing cash flow from financing activities

All the information required for this is contained in the balance sheet for the two years. There is also one entry at the end of the income statement that, if present, will also be included in this cash flow. That entry is Dividend paid. It appears after the Net Income and, strictly speaking, is not a part of the income statement itself. In the current case no dividend has been paid. The table below shows the changes in financing activities, followed by their entries in the cash flows from financing activities.

Table 7.3

Item	Nature of change	Change
Long-term debt	Decrease	$500
Common stock	Increase	$500

Note above that retained earnings does not figure as an item, as it is not a component of financing activity. It is the profit generated and retained by the company over the years. Hence, it never shows up in the cash flow statement – it is not a cash flow at all.

Cash flows from Financing activities:

Repaid long-term debt	($500	
Issued common stock	$500	
Net cash provided by financing activities		$0

Step 7 – Consolidation of all three cash flows

These three separate cash flows are consolidated into a single statement of cash flows as given below:

Statement of Cash Flows For 2020

Cash flows from Operating activities:		
Net Income		$1,490
Add depreciation expense	$460	
Gain on sale of PP&E	($100)	
Decrease in accounts receivable	$500	
Decrease in inventory	$100	
Decrease in accounts payable	($200)	
Increase in tax payable	$20	
Increase in interest payable	$20	
		$800
Net cash provided by Operating activities		$2,290
Cash flows from Investing activities:		
Sold PP&E	$540	
Net Income	($1,700)	
Net cash used in Investing activities		($1,160)
Cash flows from Financing activities:		
Repaid long-term debt	($500)	
Issued common stock	$500)	
Net cash provided by financing activities		$0
Net increase in cash		$1,130
Beginning cash balance		$500
Ending cash balance		$1,630

The final value of the ending cash balance should match with the value in 2020 balance sheet Cash. Beginning cash balance comes from Cash shown in the balance sheet from 2019.

CASE STUDY:
Case on Statement of Cash Flows – Groters Corporation

Cash inflow and outflow data for Groter's Corporation is as given below.

Cash inflows

Payments from customers	$276,000	
Loan proceed	$240,000	
Stock sale	$180,000	
Sales of equipment	$66,000	
		$762,000

Cash outflows

Inventory purchase	$211,200	
Operating expenses	$62,400	
Interest payments	$40,800	
Income tax	$37,800	
Dividends	$52,800	
Equipment purchase	$276,000	
		$681,000
		$81,000

Case Assignment

i. Prepare a statement of cash flows using the information given above. Use the direct method for statement creation.

ii. Which presentation of the cash flows is more informative – the one given above or the one in your statement of cash flows? Why is that?

Case on Statement of Cash Flows – Bumble Company

The Bumble Company has a net income of $275,000 for the current year. During the year, the following changes took place:

a. Supplies decreased by $2,000

b. Prepaid insurance increased by $1,400

c. Accounts payable decreased by $8,000

d. Accounts receivable increased by $45,000

e. Depreciation for the year is $9,000.

Case Assignment

i. Determine how the above changes would affect the cash flows from operating activities.

ii. Make a cash flow statement only for cash flows from operating activities using the data given above, using the indirect method.

Solved Examples

1. XYZ Inc. has the following transactions:

   a. Paid suppliers

   b. Sold plant

   c. Paid dividend

   d. Purchased a 90-day treasury bill

   e. Issued equity shares

   Classify them under the following:

   i.   Operating activity

   ii.   Investing activity

   iii. Financing activity

   iv.   Non-cash activity

   v.   None of the above

Solution:

   a. **Paid suppliers** – Operating activity

   b. **Sold plant** – Investing activity

   c. **Paid dividend** – Financing activity

   d. **Purchased a 90-day treasury bill** – Operating activity

   e. **Issued equity shares** – Financing activity

2. Balance sheet and income statements for ABC Inc. are given below. Prepare a Statement of Cash Flows.

Balance Sheet	2020	2019
Current assets:		
Cash and bank balances	$25	$20
Current investments	$10	$5
Inventories	$160	$138
Accounts receivable	$120	$115
Loans and advances	$50	$60
Long-term assets:		
Long-term investments	$20	$20
Fixed assets	$550	$495
Total assets	$935	$853
Current liabilities:		
Short-term provisions	$150	$138
Long-term liabilities:		
Secured loans	$180	$160
Unsecured loan	$100	$100
Stockholders' equity:		
Paid-in capital	$125	$125
Retained earnings	$380	$330
Total liabilities and equity	$935	$853

Income Statement For 2020

Sales	$1,065.00
Cost of goods sold	$805.00
Gross profit	$260.00
Depreciation	$50.00
Selling, general, and administrative expenses	$40.00
Profit before interest and tax	$170.00
Interest	$35.00
Profit before tax	$135.00
Tax	$50.00
Net Income	$85.00
Dividends	$35.00

Solution:

One point to note here is that there are no Notes to Financial Statements given. Hence, we assume that only new PP&E has been bought as they have increased in value. Now, in order to find out how much new PP&E has been bought we need to find the difference between 2020 value of fixed assets and 2019 value of fixed assets. To this, we should add the depreciation expense for 2020 as that would give us the gross fixed asset value. Below is the calculation.

New PP&E = $550 - $495 + $50 = $105

Statement of Cash Flows For 2020

Cash flows from Operating activities:

Net Income		$85
Add depreciation expense	$50	
Increase in current investments	($5)	
Increase in inventories	($22)	
Increase in accounts receivable	($5)	
Decrease in loans and advances	$10	
Increase in short term provisions	$12	
		$40
Net cash provided by Operating activities		$125
Cash flows from Investing activities:		
Purchased PP&E	($105)	
Net cash used in Investing activities		($105)
Cash flows from Financing activities:		
Took secured loans	$20	
Paid dividends	($35)	
Net cash provided by financing activities		($15)
Net increase in cash		$5
Beginning cash balance		$20
Ending cash balance		$25

Practice Exercise

1. XYZ Inc. has the following transactions:

   a. Redeemed debentures

   b. Received interest on debentures

   c. Received dividend on equity investments

   d. Obtained a computer on lease

   e. Paid interest

   f. Purchased an office

   g. Exchanged land for equity in a subsidiary

   Classify them under the following:

   i.   Operating activity

   ii.   Investing activity

   iii. Financing activity

   iv.   Non-cash activity

   v.   None of the above

2. During the year 2020, the following changes occurred in the current assets and liabilities of ABC Inc.

   a. Prepaid insurance increased by $5,000

   b. Accounts receivable reduced by $20,000

   c. Inventory of raw materials increased by $2,000

   d. Accounts payable decreased by $6,500

Depreciation for the year was $10,000 and the Net Income stood at $50,000. There were no gains or losses from any sale of PP&E. Use this data to create a statement of cash flows from operating activities.

3. Balance sheet and income statements for ZZZ Inc. are given below. It is further given that PP&E worth $500 was purchased during the year. Prepare a Statement of Cash Flows.

Balance Sheet	2020	2019
Current assets:		
Cash and bank balances	$1,180	$550
Inventories	$450	$500
Accounts receivable	$400	$200
Long-term assets:		
Fixed assets	$2,200	$1,850
Total assets	$4,230	$3,100
Current liabilities:		
Accounts payable	$400	$300
Short-term loans	$180	$300
Long-term liabilities:		
Long-term loan	$750	$500
Stockholders' equity:		
Preferred stock	$200	$100
Paid-in capital	$600	$400
Retained earnings	$2,100	$1,500
Total liabilities and equity	$4,230	$3,100

Income Statement For 2020

Sales	$3,000.00
Cost of goods sold	$1,500.00
Gross profit	$1,500.00
Depreciation	$150.00
Selling, general, and administrative expenses	$100.00
Profit before interest and tax	$1,250.00
Interest	$75.00
Profit before tax	$1,175.00
Tax	$175.00
Net Income	$1,000.00
Dividends	$400.00

Solutions to the above questions can be downloaded from the **Online Resources** *section of this book on* **www.vibrantpublishers.com**

Chapter Summary

◆ Cash Flows are the only realistic part of financial statements, as they do not contain any assumptions or estimates.

◆ Cash Flows are divided into three categories – cash flow due to operating activities, cash flow due to investing activities, and cash flow due to financing activities.

◆ Any cash inflow or outflow from the company's regular business activities is called Operating Cash flow. All activities related to long-term assets and investments are the Investing Cash Flow. All financing activities are seen under Financing Cash Flow.

◆ Cash Flow pattern depends on the type of company. For a start-up, most of the cash inflow is from financing activities. For a steady-state company and a cash-cow, most of the cash inflow is from operating activities.

◆ Cash Flow Statement can be prepared using Direct Method and Indirect Method. Direct Method requires all financial transactions to be separated into cash and non-cash transactions (like depreciation), and also into operating, investing, and financing activities. Indirect Method uses data from the balance sheet of two years and from income statement for one year to prepare the cash flow statement. Indirect Method is the most commonly used method for preparation of this statement.

Glossary

Accounting equation – Assets = Liabilities + Equity

Accounts payable – amount the company has to pay against its credit purchase

Accounts receivable – amount the company has to receive against a credit sale

Accrued liabilities – amount that the company has already incurred but not yet paid, like accrued wages, accrued interest etc.

Accumulated depreciation – total depreciation on an asset, like building or equipment, accumulated over the years

Additional paid-in capital – amount invested by stockholders over and above the paid-in capital or the par value

Amortization – process of allocating cost of intangible assets over a period of time

Asset – something that may give future benefits due to ownership or control based on a past transaction

Balance sheet – a financial statement that gives a snapshot of a company's resources (assets), obligations (liabilities), and owners' equity

Bond – an agreement between a seller and buyer where the seller agrees to repay the buyer an amount on maturity along with interest payments, either in instalments or at the end

Bookkeeping – preservation of a systematic, quantitative record of financial transactions

Cash – currency notes, coins and balance in bank accounts

Cash dividends – profit distribution to company's stockholders based on number of shares held

Common stock – a certificate representing ownership in a corporation. It gives voting rights and share in the profit of the company.

Corporation – a separate legal entity created by the state, owned by one or more persons, and having rights, privileges, and obligations that are distinct from those of its owners

Cost of goods sold – cost of manufacturing or buying an item that is sold in the normal course of business

Credit – a facility extended to a buyer to pay at a future date for a sale

Current assets – assets that are intended for use within one year

Current liabilities – obligations expected to be completed within one year

Current portion of long-term debt – that portion of long-term debt that is payable within one year

Depreciation – process of allocating cost of assets over a period of time based on the time in which the company receives their benefits

Direct method – a way of preparing statement of cash flows directly from financial transactions

Disclosure – method of reporting non-quantitative information in financial statements

Discontinued operations – disposal of a part of the business

Dividends – a way of distribution of profits of the company with shareholders

Earnings per share (EPS) – amount of net income associated with each share of the company

Equity – difference between assets and liabilities that reflects the money invested by the owners

Expanded accounting equation – Assets = Liabilities – Paid-in capital + (Revenues – Expenses) – Dividends

Expenses – amount consumed while transacting business by a company

Extraordinary items – gains and losses from transactions that are unusual and infrequent in nature

Financial statements – summary information of a company's performance using balance sheet, income statement, statement of cash flows, notes etc.

Generally Accepted Accounting Principles (GAAP) – set of accounting rules set by the local agency responsible for setting standards, like FASB

Goodwill – a competitive advantage enjoyed by a firm due to its intangible assets like, staff, rating, reputation etc.

Gross profit – difference between selling price and cost price of a product or service

Income from continuing operations – income generated from those operations that are expected to continue in future

Income statement – reports the net income earned by the company over the defined period, generally a quarter or year

Intangible assets – non-physical assets like, goodwill, trademark etc.

Inventory – common term used to describe stored raw materials, in-process goods and finished products until they are sold

Investment securities – composed of publicly traded stocks and bonds

Lease – a contract between two parties that temporarily gives the right over the property of one to the other over a specified period of time for a specified amount

Long-term debt – long-term loans, notes, debentures, mortgages etc.

Mortgage – a loan secured by an asset pledged to the lender

Net Income – difference between revenues and expenses

Net Loss – same as net income but when expenses are greater than revenues

Notes to financial statements – additional information provided in the financial statements

Operating income – measure of income that assesses the company's main business performance

Owners' equity – owners' share in the company

Paid-in capital – amount of money invested by the company's stockholders against shares of the company

Par value – face value of one share of the company – generally $1

Preferred stock – a class of stock that is similar to debt and provides a fixed stated return to preferred stockholders

Prepaid expenses – payment made in advance like, insurance paid for the entire year

Property, plant, and equipment – long-term assets like, land, building and machinery

Retained earnings – that portion of profits (or losses) that have been retained by the company instead of being paid as dividends to stockholders

Revenue – amount of money made by the company through its business activities, interest receipts etc.

Sales – a type of revenue made by the company in normal course of business

Shareholders – investors in a company

Statement of cash flows – a financial statement that gives all inflows and outflows of cash

Treasury stock – name given to stocks of a company when they are bought back by them

Notes